Pat Sloan's

Fast-F… QUI…

LEISURE ARTS, INC.
Little Rock, Arkansas

table of CONTENTS

Meet Pat Sloan • 3

Why Pre-Cuts? • 4

Types of Pre-Cuts • 4

Making Your Own Pre-Cuts • 5

FAQs • 6

A Box of Chocolates • 7

Welcome to the Neighborhood • 10

Boardwalk • 18

Flirt • 24

Choose Your Snooze • 34

Under the Sea • 42

Pretty Plates • 48

Bozley's Triangles • 54

I Remember • 64

General Instructions • 70

EDITORIAL STAFF
Editor-in-Chief: Susan White Sullivan
Designer Relations Director: Debra Nettles
Special Projects Director: Susan Frantz Wiles
Craft Publications Director: Cheryl Johnson
Senior Prepress Director: Mark Hawkins
Art Publications Director: Rhonda Shelby
Technical Writer: Jean Lewis
Technical Associates: Mary Hutcheson and Lisa Lancaster
Editorial Writer: Susan McManus Johnson
Art Category Manager: Lora Puls
Graphic Designer: Amy Temple
Graphic Artists: Jacob Casleton and Janie Marie Wright
Imaging Technicians: Stephanie Johnson and Mark R. Potter
Photography Director: Katherine Laughlin
Contributing Photostylist: Christy Myers
Contributing Photographer: Mark Mathews
Publishing Systems Administrator: Becky Riddle
Publishing Systems Assistants: Clint Hanson and Keiji Yumoto
MAC IT Specialist: Robert Young

BUSINESS STAFF
Vice President and Chief Operations Officer: Tom Siebenmorgen
Director of Finance and Administration: Laticia Mull Dittrich
Vice President, Sales and Marketing: Pam Stebbins
Sales Director: Martha Adams
Marketing Director: Margaret Reinold
Creative Services Director: Jeff Curtis
Information Technology Director: Hermine Linz
Controller: Francis Caple
Vice President, Operations: Jim Dittrich
Comptroller, Operations: Rob Thieme
Retail Customer Service Manager: Stan Raynor
Print Production Manager: Fred F. Pruss

Library of Congress Control Number: 2010926083 • ISBN-13: 978-1-60140-662-0 • ISBN-10: 1-60140-662-2

Hi, quilting friend!

Do pre-cut fabrics call to you? I think I can hear them when I walk in the door of a quilt shop! Neatly rolled or stacked and tied with pretty ribbons—pre-cut fabric bundles have a lure that's irresistible. I've swapped pre-cuts with members of my quilt guild and hosted a game on my Death by Quilting Web site where players exchanged squares.

Not familiar with pre-cuts? They're groups of fabric pieces that have been cut to a uniform size and shape—and they're a handy way to fast-forward your quilt-making.

Pre-cuts have been around a while, but only recently became a big trend. Just a few years ago, fabric manufacturers started bundling 5" squares called "charm packs" and rolls of $2^1/_2$" wide strips generally referred to as "jelly rolls." These contained one piece of each fabric in a designer's collection. Today, pre-cuts can include strips of various widths, several sizes of squares, or even triangles. Many quilt shops now cut and package their own pre-cuts by color or theme.

In *Fast-Forward Quilts*, I share my reasons for using pre-cuts. I walk you through the types of pre-cuts currently available, then show you how to create them from your own scraps. I also answer some of the most frequently asked questions about pre-cuts.

And of course, you get to choose from 16 fast-forward projects to make! I had so much fun designing these patterns especially for use with pre-cuts that I know you'll have a wonderful time making all your favorites!
—Pat

meet PAT SLOAN

When you see all the spirit and whimsy that Pat Sloan puts into her quilt designs and techniques, it's hard to believe she wasn't always free to quilt as she pleased. In fact, it took a big career change to put Pat where she wanted to be, professionally and creatively.

"I'm more excited about life now that I create all the time," says Pat. "I decided after 20 years of computer programming that it was time to do what makes me happy. I've been fulltime as a quilt designer and teacher since 2000, with my husband Gregg handling the business side of managing our company. My life is all about quilting, twenty-four/seven."

When Pat isn't designing fabric for P&B Textiles, writing quilt books, or developing patterns, she's maintaining her popular Web site and blog at PatSloan.com.

If you want to discover more of Pat's exciting designs and original quilt-making techniques, visit your local fabric store or LeisureArts.com to collect all of her books.

why PRE-CUTS?

I am asked this question all the time—why would I want to buy pre-cut fabric? These beautiful bundles make great decorating accessories for any sewing room or studio! And here are some even better reasons to add pre-cuts to your fabric collection:

- Take the guess work out of planning a quilt. Composed of one fabric collection or fabrics specifically selected to be used together, these bundles will be as beautiful in your quilt as they are in the stack or roll.
- Save time and effort. Some pre-cuts can be used "as is" and some will require only minor sub-cutting. Just think of the cutting steps you are eliminating!
- Build a fabric collection. If you don't have a large stash or you're missing a certain type or color of fabric, pre-cuts will do the job. I like to pick up a pre-cut bundle of 1930's prints every so often just to give me more variety for my future 30's quilt.
- Audition fabric choices before buying yardage. Having actual pieces of the fabrics makes it a lot easier to plan a quilt—it's a lot like purchasing sample cans of paint to try the colors on your wall before painting the whole room!
- Get immense variety at a super reasonable price for scrappy quilts. Also, there is usually a lot less waste.
- Add interest and excitement to an appliqué project. Instead of using just one green for leaves, a bundle of pre-cuts gives you the option of using several different greens.

types of PRE-CUTS

What's in a name?

Just say Fat Quarter and most quilters immediately know you are referring to a rectangle of fabric that is approximately 18" x 22". Other pre-cut names are not quite so easily recognized. Because fabric manufacturers choose the names for their pre-cuts, two packages of $2^1/_2$" wide strips from different manufacturers may have different names. For example, one company may call their strips Jelly Rolls while another might use the name Sushi Rolls. But names aren't nearly as important as the size of the cut. Be sure to check the size of the pre-cuts you wish to purchase against your pattern requirements.

Numbers do matter!
The number of pieces in a pre-cut bundle sometimes varies with the number of fabrics in a collection. In the table on the right, I've listed some common pre-cuts. If there is a standard number of pieces in a bundle, that number has been included. Always check the number of pieces in a pre-cut against your pattern requirements.

NAME	CUT SIZE	PIECES
Fat Quarter Bundles	approx. 18" x 22"	varies
Fat Eighth Bundles	approx. 9" x 22"	varies
Petit Fours	2 1/2" x 2 1/2"	160 squares from 4 collections
Charm Packs	5" x 5" or 5 1/2" x 5 1/2"	varies
Layer Cakes	10" x 10"	40 squares
Jelly Rolls	2 1/2" x width of fabric	40 strips
Honey Buns	1 1/2" x width of fabric	40 strips
Dessert Rolls	5" x width of fabric	10 strips
Bali Pops	2 1/2" x width of fabric	40 strips
Sushi Rolls	2 7/8" x width of fabric	40-45 strips
Twice The Charms	5 1/2" x 22"	varies
Turnovers	6" x 6" x 8 1/2"	80 triangles
Jelly Cakes	mixed	1 Jelly Roll and 1 Layer Cake
Charming Jelly Cake	mixed	1 charm Pack, 1 Jelly Roll and 1 Layer Cake
Sweet Box	mixed	1 Honey Bun from 2 different collections

making your own PRE-CUTS

Why would anyone want to make pre-cuts?
Cutting your leftover fabric pieces into squares, strips, and triangles is a thrifty way to build a collection of ready-to-use pre-cuts. And, you've already used those fabrics in another project so you know they go together—no guesswork!

Getting Started
Now that you have decided to give pre-cuts a try, think about the following questions:

- What are the most useful size(s) and shape(s) for you. Small squares? Large squares? Strips? Maybe it's all of these!

- How many pre-cuts do you think you will make? Do you make a lot of quilts? Do you have a lot of scraps?

- Next, decide how you want to sort the shapes. I think the best way to sort ALL fabric is by color. With multi-color prints, go with the FIRST color you see when you look at the fabric. It may not be the background color, but it's most likely the dominant one (see my book *"Take the Fear Out Of Color"* for more thoughts on color).

Once you have an idea of the size, shape, and number of pre-cuts you may have, and you've made a plan for sorting, the next step is storage.

Storage of Pre-cuts

A good storage system is key because you need to be able to find and use your pre-cuts easily.

- Think about the types of containers you will need to store your pre-cuts. How do you store other fabric pieces? On shelves? In bins, tubs, or baskets? You will need containers that will accommodate the size, shape, and number of pre-cuts you may have AND can be stored close to your other fabric pieces of the same color.

  For example, if you store fabric folded on a shelf, use a bin/tub/basket for your pre-cuts that fits on the shelf next to the stack. Then, when you pull green fabric for a quilt, also pull the container of green pre-cuts. Simple!

- If you pre-cut a LOT of scraps, you may find that you will need a container for each shape as well as color of pre-cuts. For example, you may have a bin of yellow 5" x 5" squares, one of yellow 2$^1/_2$" strips, and another of yellow 10" x 10" squares, etc.

Cutting Scraps In A Timely Manner

I urge you get into the habit of making and storing your pre-cuts as you cut the pieces for a project. I have two methods that seem to work for most people.

- The first is the most obvious. Have your storage containers handy. As you create a scrap, immediately cut it to the desired shape. Put it in the right container and you're done!

- My method is to hook a SMALL bag onto the end of my cutting table to hold scraps. When this SMALL bag (did I tell you it was SMALL?) starts getting full, I cut the scraps into shapes and put them away.

FAQ's

If you are a newcomer to the world of pre-cuts you may find these frequently asked questions and answers helpful.

Q: Should I pre-wash pre-cuts?
A: Most people do not pre-wash because pre-cuts are delicate and may distort when washed. If you feel you must pre-wash, for example, to keep dark colors from running, hand rinse the pieces in cool water. Lay them flat on a towel and pat to remove excess water. Gently smooth the pieces; air dry and press. **Note:** Fabrics that are not pre-washed may shrink slightly if you wash the finished project, giving them an "antiqued" appearance.

Q: Some pre-cuts have pinked edges, should I trim those off?
A: No, leave the pinked edges. Most manufacturers include the points in the measurements given on the package. For example, the measurement across a 10" square, from one outside point to the opposite outside point is usually 10".

Q: If the edges are pinked, how do I know if I am sewing an accurate $^1/_4$" seam?
A: Measure your shape as described above. If it measures exactly 10", align the tip of the points with your $^1/_4$" seam guide. If your shape is larger or smaller, take a scant or deep $^1/_4$"seam allowance accordingly.

Q: Do you ever sub-cut pre-cuts?
A: Yes, in fact some of the projects in this book call for the pre-cuts to be sub-cut. Your project instructions will tell you what size to cut each piece.

Q: You've mentioned swapping pre-cuts, how do I get started?
A: Choose a size, color, or theme of pre-cuts you want to swap. Ask your quilting friends to join you in a swap, or organize a group in your quilt guild, or look on the internet for quilt groups like my Death By Quilting.

Now, armed with your knowledge of pre-cuts, you are ready to choose your favorite project and get started making a fun and fabulous quilt!

a box of CHOCOLATES

This little quilt provides the perfect introduction to working with pre-cut fabrics. It comes together really quickly! You can hang it on the wall or use it as a table topper—such a cool way to use a single charm pack in holiday or everyday prints. Isn't it yummy?

Version One
Instructions begin on page 8.

Finished Size: 21" x 21" (53 cm x 53 cm)
Finished Block Size: 12" x 12" (30 cm x 30 cm)

fabric requirements

*Yardage is based on 43"/44" (109 cm/112 cm) wide fabric. Instructions given are for Version 1. Changes for Version 2 are noted with an *.*

1 Charm Pack ***or*** 34 assorted squares 5" x 5" (13 cm x 13 cm) for quilt top and binding
Two $5^3/_8$" x $5^3/_8$" (14 cm x 14 cm) squares of fabric for inner corner triangles
25" x 25" (64 cm x 64 cm) square of fabric for backing

You will also need:
25" x 25" (64 cm x 64 cm) piece of batting

organizing the pre-cuts

The key to making this little quilt is to sort your squares into colors, play with the arrangement until you are happy, and then make sure you have enough pieces of each color for each section of the quilt top. Sometimes you may need to add in a square or two of fabric from your stash to make it work and that's OK!

From Charm Pack or assorted squares:

- Select 6 light squares for Triangle-Squares.
- Select 6 dark squares for Triangle-Squares.
- Select 8 dark and 6 light squares for border squares and border triangles.*
- Select 8 squares for binding.

* For Version 2, select 8 light and 8 dark squares for border squares.

cutting the pieces

All measurements include $^1/_4$" seam allowances. As you cut, keep pieces separated by using sandwich bags, envelopes, or pins and label each packet.

From light squares for Triangle-Squares:

- Cut each square in half twice to make 4 **light small squares** $2^1/_2$" x $2^1/_2$" (24 total, will use 22). Trim 2 of the light small squares to $2^3/_8$" x $2^3/_8$". Cut these 2 squares in half once diagonally to make 4 **light small triangles**.

From dark squares for Triangle-Squares:

- Cut each square in half twice to make 4 **dark small squares** $2^1/_2$" x $2^1/_2$" (24 total). Trim 4 of the dark small squares to $2^3/_8$" x $2^3/_8$". Cut these 4 squares in half once diagonally to make 8 **dark small triangles**.

From light and dark squares for border squares and border triangles:

- Trim each square to $4^1/_2$" x $4^1/_2$". Cut 2 of the squares in half once diagonally to make 4 **border triangles**.*

From squares for binding:

- Cut 24 **strips** $1^1/_2$" wide.

From squares for inner corner triangles:

- Cut squares in half once diagonally to make 4 **inner corner triangles**.

* For Version 2, do not cut squares in half.

making the block

*Follow **Piecing And Pressing**, page 71, to make the Block. Match right sides and use 1/4" seam allowances throughout. **Note:** You will be working with very small pieces, be sure to use an accurate seam allowance.*

1. Draw a diagonal line on wrong side of each **light small square**.
2. With right sides together, place a light small square on top of a **dark small square**. Stitch seam 1/4" from each side of drawn line (FIG. 1).
3. Cut along drawn line and press open to make 2 TRIANGLE-SQUARES. Make 40 Triangle-Squares. Trim Triangle-Squares to 2" x 2".
4. Referring to **Block Center Diagram** for placement, arrange and then sew Triangle-Squares and **light** and **dark small triangles** together to make BLOCK CENTER.
5. Sew 1**inner corner triangle** to each long edge of Block Center to make BLOCK.

assembling the quilt top

Before sewing, arrange the border squares and border triangles around the Block to check color placement.

1. Sew 3 **border squares** together to make TOP/BOTTOM BORDER. Make 2 Top/Bottom borders. Sew Top/Bottom borders to opposite sides of Block.
2. Sew 3 border squares and 2 **border triangles** together to make SIDE BORDER. Make 2 Side Borders. Sew Side Borders to Block.

completing the quilt

1. Follow **Quilting**, page 74, to layer and quilt as desired. My quilt is machine quilted with a large echoing flower in the center and a leaf in each inner corner triangle. There is a flower and leaf pattern in the border.
2. Refer to **Making A Hanging Sleeve**, page 75, to make and attach a hanging sleeve, if desired.
3. Use **binding strips** and follow **Making Single-Fold Binding**, page 76, to make **binding**. Follow **Pat's Machine-Sewn Binding**, page 78, to bind quilt.

FIG. 1

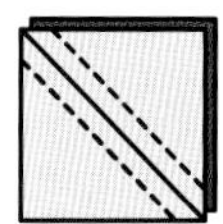

TRIANGLE-SQUARE (MAKE 40)

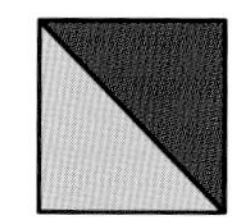

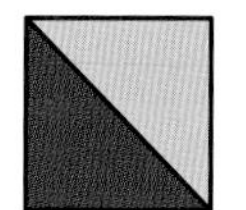

BLOCK CENTER

BLOCK

TOP/BOTTOM BORDER (MAKE 2)

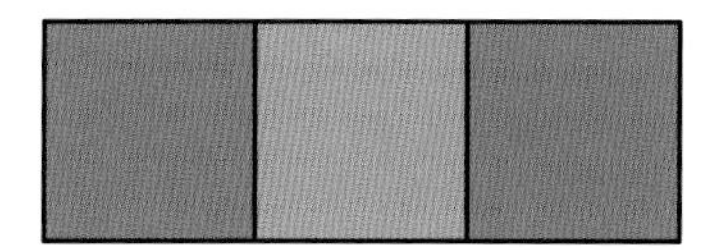

SIDE BORDERS (MAKE 2)

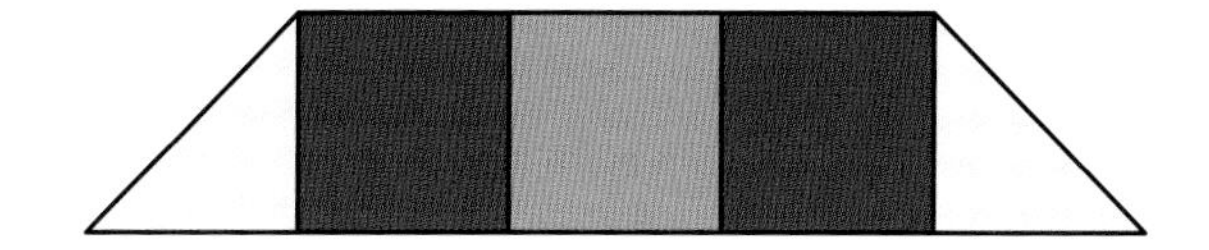

VERSION 2

welcome to the **NEIGHBORHOOD**

Wouldn't you love to go for a walk in this neighborhood? The red floral and rich brown print fabrics go together like raspberries and chocolate. Or like a cake in those flavors—a 10" layer cake, most specifically. What delicious colors can you imagine using for this pattern? I can see orange with brown or yellow with blue. How about decorating your little neighborhood for Christmas by using your favorite holiday pre-cuts?

Finished Size: 41$^1/_2$" x 41$^1/_2$" (105 cm x 105 cm)
Finished Block Size: 9$^1/_2$" x 9$^1/_2$" (24 cm x 24 cm)

fabric requirements

Yardage is based on 43"/44" (109 cm/112 cm) wide fabric.

1 Layer Cake ***or*** 34 assorted squares 10" x 10" (25 cm x 25 cm)
$^5/_8$ yd (57 cm) of pink print
2$^5/_8$ yds (2.4 m) of fabric for backing

You will also need:

45$^1/_2$" x 45$^1/_2$" (116 cm x 116 cm) piece of batting

organizing the pre-cuts

From Layer Cake or assorted squares:

- Select 5 light squares for backgrounds.
- Select 3 medium squares for windows/doors.
- Select 3 medium squares for Nine-Patch blocks.
- Set aside remaining light/medium squares for binding.
- Select 5 dark squares for roofs/sashings.
- Select 9 dark squares for houses.
- Select 4 dark squares for Nine-Patch blocks/sashings.

cutting the pieces

*Follow **Rotary Cutting**, page 70 to cut fabric. For the most efficient use of the fabric squares, refer to **Cutting Diagrams**, page 17. All measurements include 1/4" seam allowances. As you cut, keep pieces separated by using sandwich bags, envelopes, or pins and label each packet.*

From *each* light square for backgrounds:

- Cut 2 **large background rectangles** 2 1/2" x 5 1/2" (10 total, will use 9).
- Cut 2 **medium background rectangles** 2 1/2" x 3 1/2" (10 total, will use 9).
- Cut 2 **small background rectangles** 1 1/2" x 2" (10 total, will use 9).
- Cut 2 squares 3" x 3". Cut each square in half once diagonally to make 20 **background triangles** (will use 18).

From *each* medium square for windows/doors:

- Cut 3 **windows** 3" x 4" (9 total).
- Cut 3 **doors** 2 1/2" x 5" (9 total).

From medium squares for Nine-Patch blocks:

- Cut a *total* of 12 **strips** 1 1/2" x 10".

From light/medium squares for binding and any light/medium scraps:

- Cut 24 **binding strips** 1 1/2" x 10".

From *each* of 3 dark squares for roofs/sashings:

- Cut 3 **roofs** 2 1/2" x 4".
- Cut 3 squares 3" x 3". Cut each square in half once diagonally to make 18 **roof triangles**.
- Cut 2 **sashing strips** 1 1/2" x 10" (6 total).

From *each* of the 2 remaining dark squares for roofs/sashings:

- Cut 6 **sashing strips** 1 1/2" x 10" (12 total).

From *each* dark square for houses:

- Cut 2 **fronts** 1 1/2" x 6" (18 total).
- Cut 2 **small sides** 1 1/2" x 6" (18 total).
- Cut 1 **large side** 2" x 6" (9 total).
- Cut 2 **window facings** 3" x 1 1/2" (18 total).
- Cut 1 **door facing** 2 1/2" x 1 1/2" (9 total).
- Cut 1 **chimney** 2" x 1 1/2" (9 total).
- Cut 2 **squares** 3" x 3". Cut each square in half once diagonally to make 18 **front triangles**.

From dark squares for Nine-Patch blocks/ sashings:

- Cut a *total* of 15 **strips** 1 1/2" x 10".
- Cut a *total* of 24 **sashing strips** 1 1/2" x 10".

From pink print:

- Cut 12 strips 1 1/2" wide. From these strips, cut 48 **sashing strips** 1 1/2" x 10".

CHIMNEY UNIT

UNIT 1

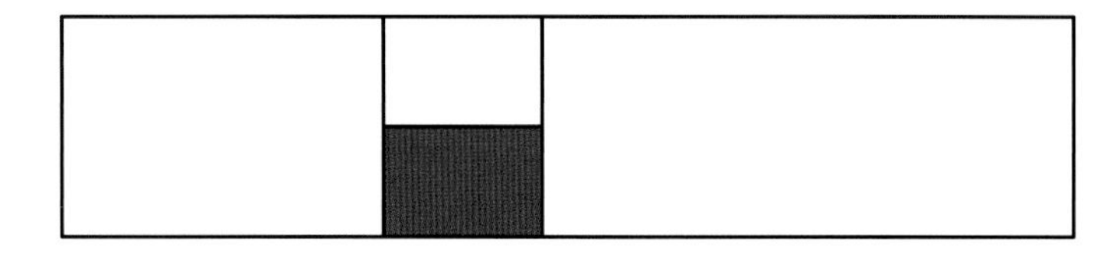

TRIANGLE-SQUARE A

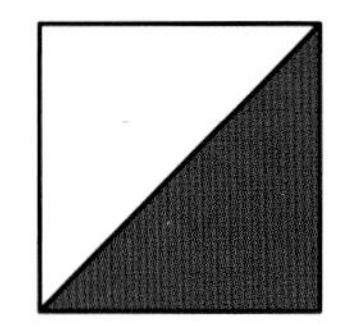

TRIANGLE-SQUARE B

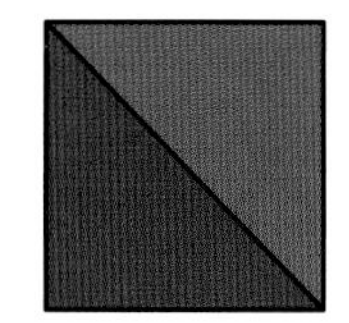

TRIANGLE-SQUARE C

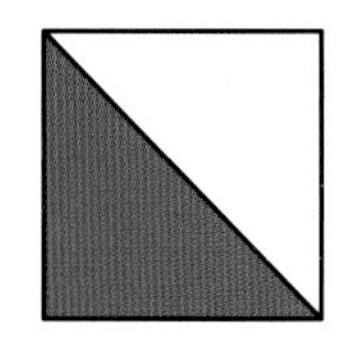

UNIT 2

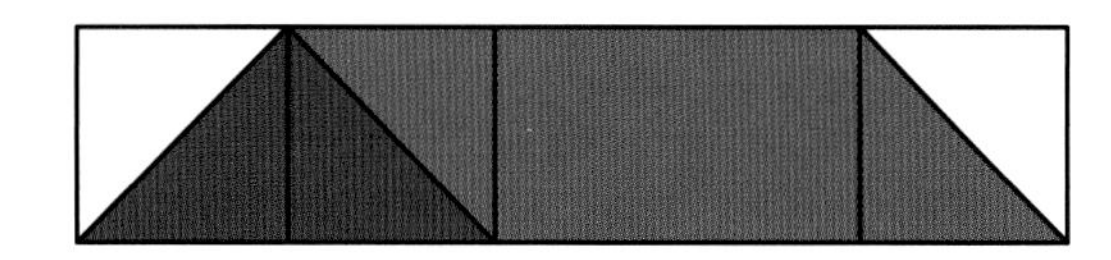

WINDOW UNIT

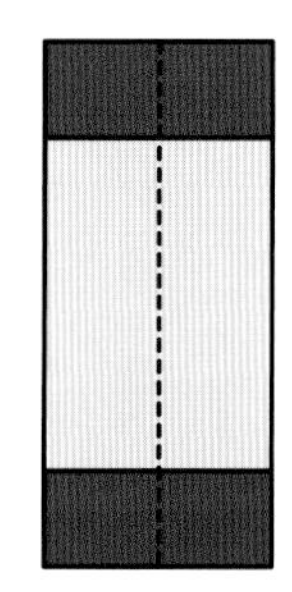

DOOR UNIT

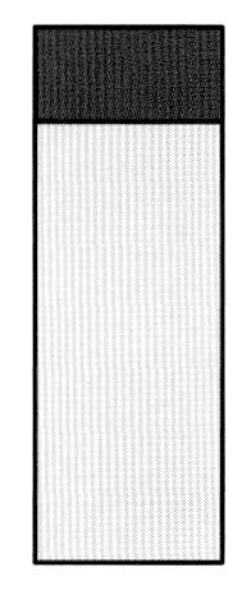

making the blocks

*Follow **Piecing And Pressing**, page 71, to make the Blocks. Match right sides and use $^{1}/_{4}$" seam allowances throughout.*

house block

Tip: Layer Cakes usually contain several of the same print in different colorways. To avoid repeating prints within a block, I like to select and then arrange the pieces of each block on my design wall before beginning to sew.

For each block from like fabrics, you will need the pieces listed under each bullet:

- 1 **large background rectangle**, 1 **medium background rectangle**, 1 **small background rectangle**, and 2 **background triangles**.
- 1 **window** and 1 **door**.
- 2 **fronts**, 1 **door facing**, 2 **front triangles**, and 1 **chimney**.
- 2 **small sides**, 1 **large side**, and 2 **window facings**.
- 1 **roof** and 2 **roof triangles**.

1. Sew **small background rectangle** and **chimney** together to make CHIMNEY UNIT.
2. Sew Chimney Unit, **medium background rectangle**, and **large background rectangle** together to make UNIT 1.
3. Sew 1 **background triangle** and 1 **front triangle** together to make TRIANGLE-SQUARE A. Trim Triangle-Square A to $2^{1}/_{2}$" x $2^{1}/_{2}$".
4. Sew 1 **front triangle** and 1 **roof triangle** together to make TRIANGLE-SQUARE B. Trim Triangle-Square B to $2^{1}/_{2}$" x $2^{1}/_{2}$".
5. Sew 1 **background triangle** and 1 **roof triangle** together to make TRIANGLE-SQUARE C. Trim Triangle-Square C to $2^{1}/_{2}$" x $2^{1}/_{2}$".
6. Sew **Triangle-Squares A** and **B**, **roof**, and **Triangle-Square C** together to make UNIT 2.
7. Sew 1 **window facing** to each short edge of 1 **window** to make WINDOW UNIT. Cut Window Unit in half lengthwise to make 2 SMALL WINDOW UNITS.
8. Sew 1 **door facing** to one short edge of **door** to make DOOR UNIT.

9. Sew 2 **fronts**, Door Unit, 2 **small sides**, **large side,** and 2 Small Window Units together to make UNIT 3.
10. Sew Units 1, 2, and 3 together to make HOUSE BLOCK. Make 9 **House Blocks**.

nine-patch blocks

1. Matching long edges, sew 1 **dark** and 2 **medium strips** together to make STRIP SET A. Make 3 Strip Set A's.
2. Cut across each Strip Set A at $1^1/_2$" intervals to make UNIT 4's. Make 16 Unit 4's.
3. Matching long edges, sew 1 **medium** and 2 **dark strips** together to make STRIP SET B. Make 6 Strip Set B's.
4. Cut across each Strip Set B at $1^1/_2$" intervals to make UNIT 5's. Make 32 Unit 5's.
5. Sew 1 Unit 4 and 2 Unit 5's together to make NINE-PATCH BLOCK. Make 16 Nine-Patch Blocks.

UNIT 3

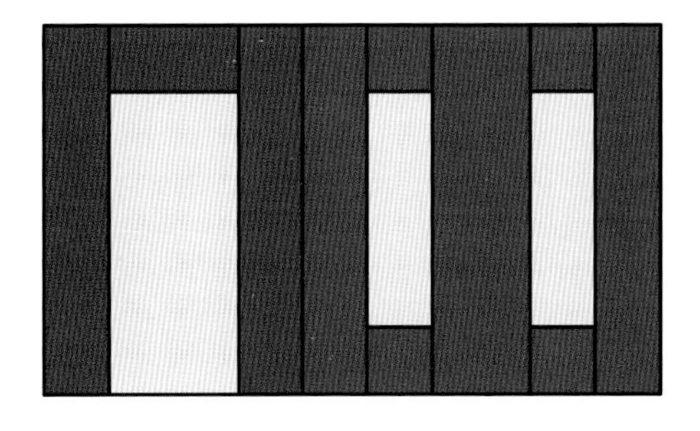

HOUSE BLOCK (MAKE 9)

STRIP SET A (MAKE 3) **UNIT 4** (MAKE 16)

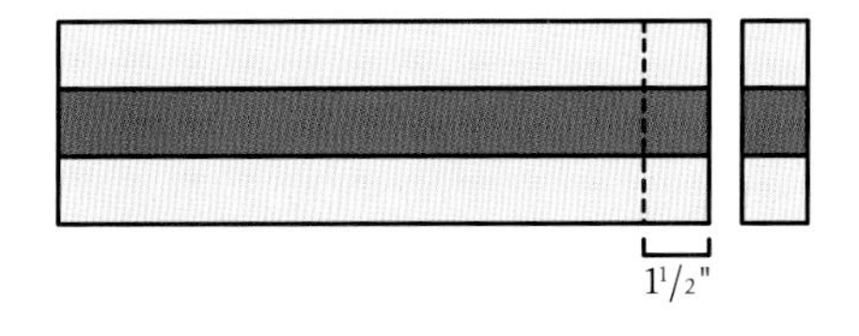

STRIP SET B (MAKE 6) **UNIT 5** (MAKE 32)

NINE-PATCH BLOCK (MAKE 16)

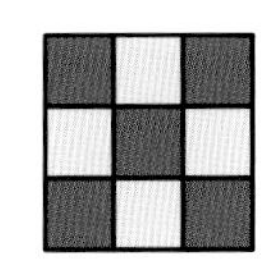

assembling the quilt top

Refer to QUILT TOP DIAGRAM for placement.

1. Matching long edges, sew 1 **dark** and 2 **pink print sashing strips** together to make SASHING UNIT. Make 24 Sashing Units.
2. Sew 4 Sashing Units and 3 House Blocks together to make ROW. Make 3 Rows.
3. Sew 3 Sashing Units and 4 Nine-Patch Blocks together to make SASHING ROW. Make 3 Sashing Rows.
4. Sew Rows and Sashing Rows together to make QUILT TOP.

completing the quilt

1. Follow **Quilting**, page 74, to layer and quilt as desired. My quilt is machine quilted with scallops on the roofs and outline quilting around all the remaining sections of the houses. There are swirls of smoke coming out of the chimneys and a leaf and vine pattern in the sashings.
2. Refer to **Making A Hanging Sleeve**, page 75, to make and attach a hanging sleeve, if desired.
3. Use **binding strips** and follow **Making Single-Fold Binding**, page 76, to make **binding**. Follow **Attaching Binding**, page 76, to bind quilt.

SASHING UNIT (MAKE 24)

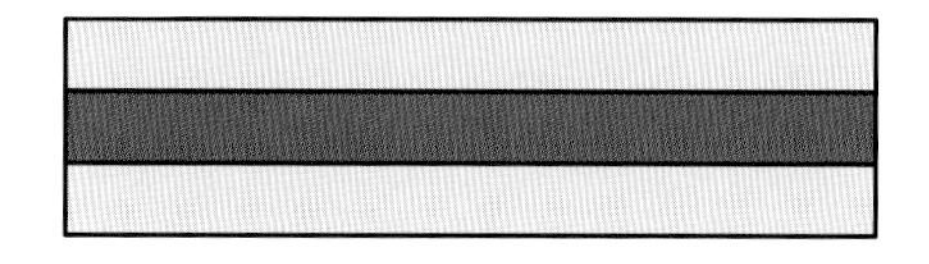

ROW (MAKE 3)

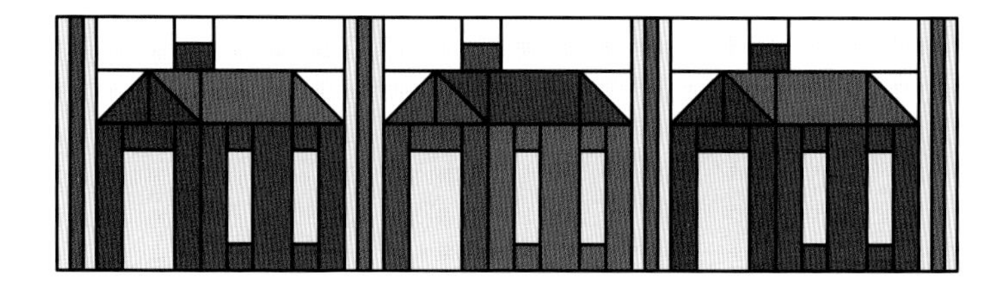

SASHING ROW (MAKE 4)

QUILT TOP DIAGRAM

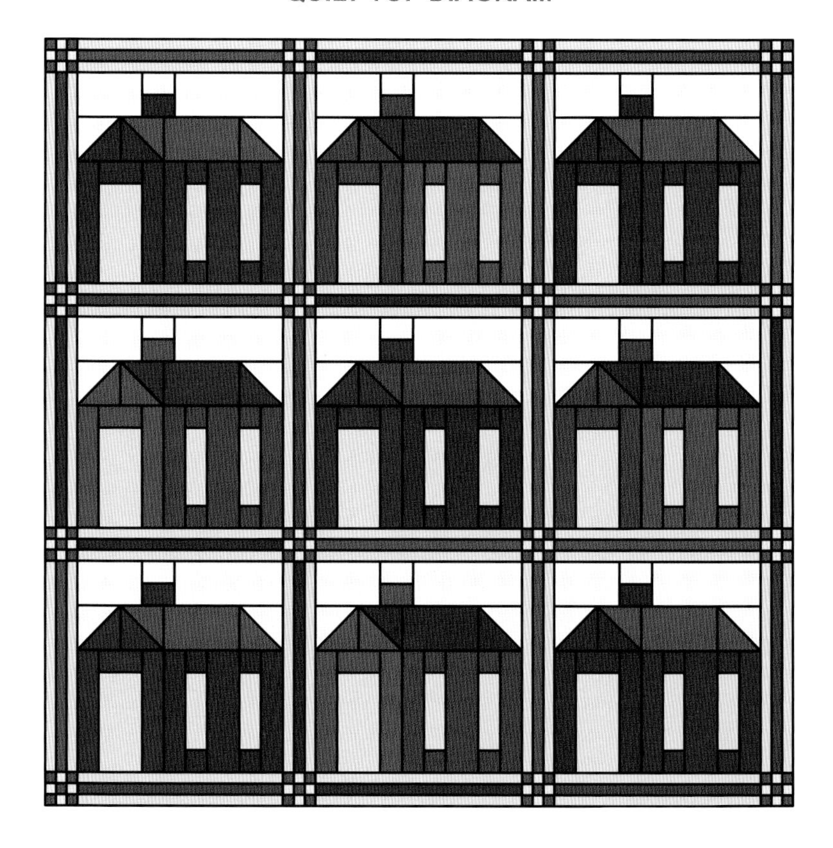

Background Cutting Diagram
(use 5 light 10" x 10" squares)

Medium Background Rectangle 2 1/2" x 3 1/2"

Medium Background Rectangle 2 1/2" x 3 1/2"

Small Background Rectangles 1 1/2" x 2"

Background Triangle Cut 3" x 3" square; cut once diagonally

Background Triangle Cut 3" x 3" square; cut once diagonally

Large Background Rectangle 2 1/2" x 5 1/2"

Large Background Rectangle 2 1/2" x 5 1/2"

Doors and Windows Cutting Diagram
(use 3 medium 10" x 10" squares)

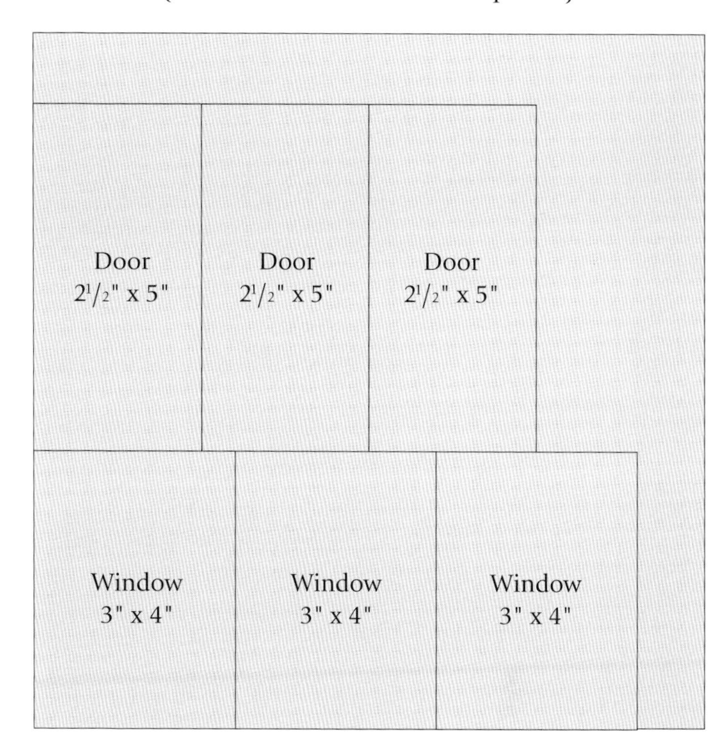

Roof and Sashing Strips Cutting Diagram
(use 3 dark 10" x 10" squares)

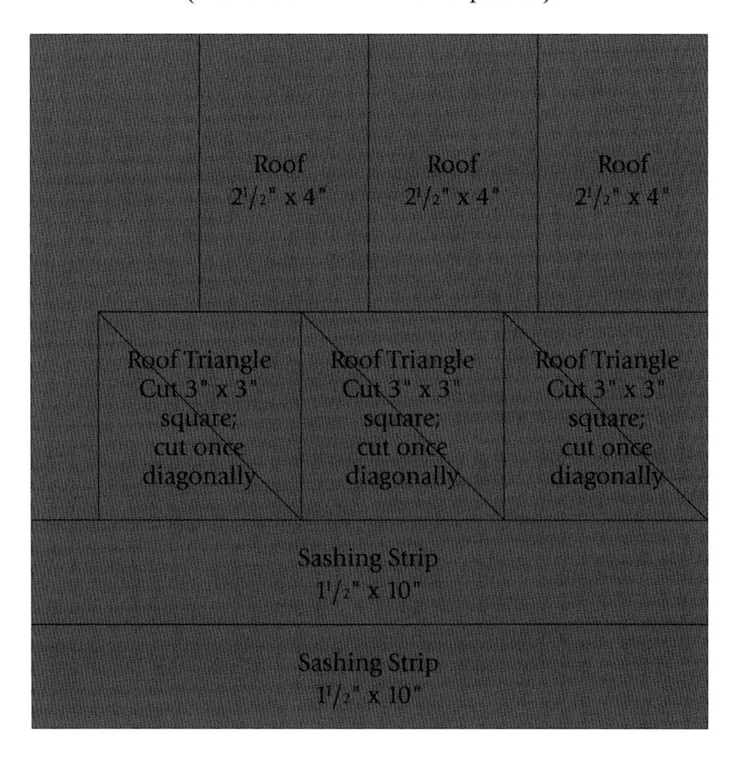

Houses Cutting Diagram
(use 9 dark 10" x 10" squares)

Door Facing 2 1/2" x 1 1/2"

Front Triangle Cut 3" x 3" square; cut once diagonally

Front Triangle Cut 3" x 3" square; cut once diagonally

Chimney 2" x 1 1/2"

Window Facing 3" x 1 1/2"

Window Facing 3" x 1 1/2"

Front 1 1/2" x 6"

Front 1 1/2" x 6"

Small Side 1 1/2" x 6"

Small Side 1 1/2" x 6"

Large Side 2" x 6"

boardwalk

Several quilts in this collection remind me of warm weather activities. This one is definitely a trip to the seaside, where we can stroll on the boardwalk and eat saltwater taffy, hot dogs, and funnel cakes. I do believe making this colorful quilt may be the most summertime fun you can have without the sand and calories!

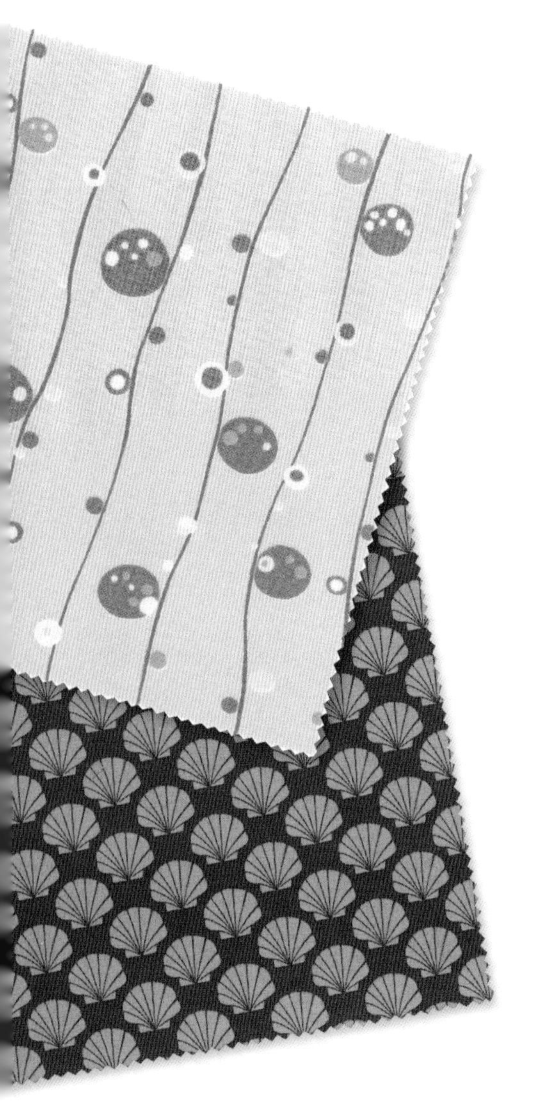

Finished Size: 53" x 67" (135 cm x 170 cm)
Finished Block Size: 12" x 12" (30 cm x 30 cm)

fabric requirements

Yardage is based on 43"/44" (109 cm/112 cm) wide fabric.

1 Charm Pack ***or*** 28 assorted squares 5" x 5" (13 cm x 13 cm) for blocks
1 Jelly Roll ***or*** 31 assorted strips $2^1/_2$" x 40" (6 cm x 102 cm) for blocks, borders, and binding
1 yd (91 cm) of teal tone-on-tone for blocks and border
$^7/_8$ yd (80 cm) of yellow print for sashings
$4^1/_8$ yds (3.8 m) of fabric for backing

You will also need:

61" x 75" (155 cm x 191 cm) piece of batting

organizing the pre-cuts

From Charm Pack or assorted squares:

- Select 12 blue squares for Triangle-Squares.
- Select 12 green squares for Triangle-Squares.
- Select 4 red squares for border corners.

From Jelly Roll or assorted strips:

- Select 2 red strips for sashing squares.
- Select 22 strips for border rectangles and block squares.
- Select 7 strips for binding.

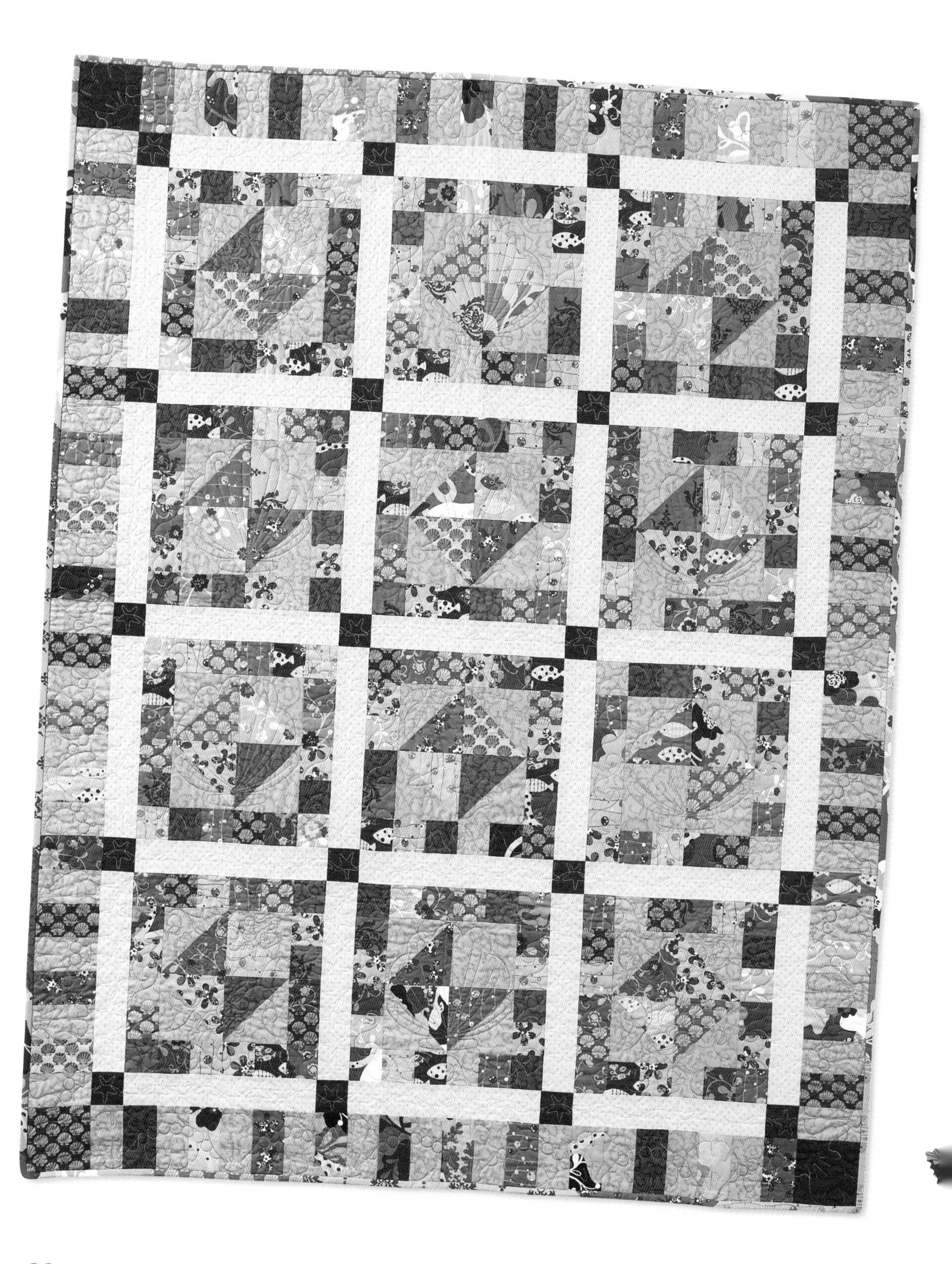

cutting the pieces

*Follow **Rotary Cutting**, page 70, to cut fabric. Cut all strips from the selvage-to-selvage width of the fabric. All measurements include ¼" seam allowances. As you cut, keep pieces separated by using sandwich bags, envelopes, or pins and label each packet.*

From red strips for sashing squares:

- Cut 20 red **sashing squares** 2½" x 2½".

From strips for border rectangles and block squares:

- Cut 50 assorted **border rectangles** 2½" x 4½".
- Cut 240 assorted **small squares** 2½" x 2½".

From teal tone-on-tone:

- Cut 3 strips 5" wide. From these strips, cut 24 **squares** 5" x 5".
- Cut 7 strips 2½" wide. From these strips, cut 52 **border rectangles** 2½" x 4½".

From yellow print:

- Cut 11 strips 2½" wide. From these strips, cut 31 **sashings** 2½" x 12½".

making the blocks

*Follow **Piecing And Pressing**, page 71, to make the Blocks. Match right sides and use ¼" seam allowances throughout.*

1. Draw a diagonal line on wrong side of each teal **square**.
2. With right sides together, place 1 teal **square** on top of 1 green **square**. Stitch seam ¼" from each side of drawn line (FIG. 1).
3. Cut along drawn line and press open to make 2 TRIANGLE-SQUARE A's. Make 24 Triangle-Square A's. Trim Triangle-Square A's to 4½" x 4½".
4. Repeat Steps 2 and 3 using teal and blue **squares** to make 24 TRIANGLE-SQUARE B's.
5. Sew 2 Triangle-Square A's and 2 Triangle-Square B's together to make BLOCK CENTER. Make 12 Block Centers.

FIG. 1

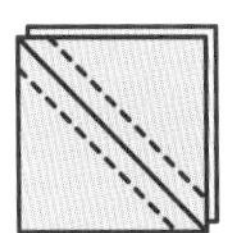

TRIANGLE-SQUARE A (MAKE 24)

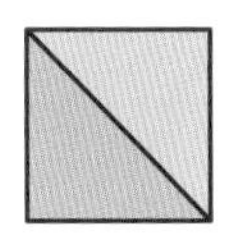
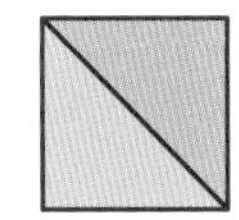

TRIANGLE-SQUARE B (MAKE 24)

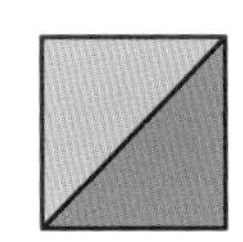
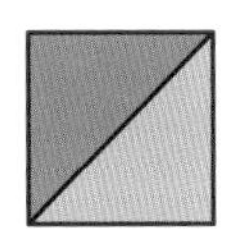

BLOCK CENTER (MAKE 12)

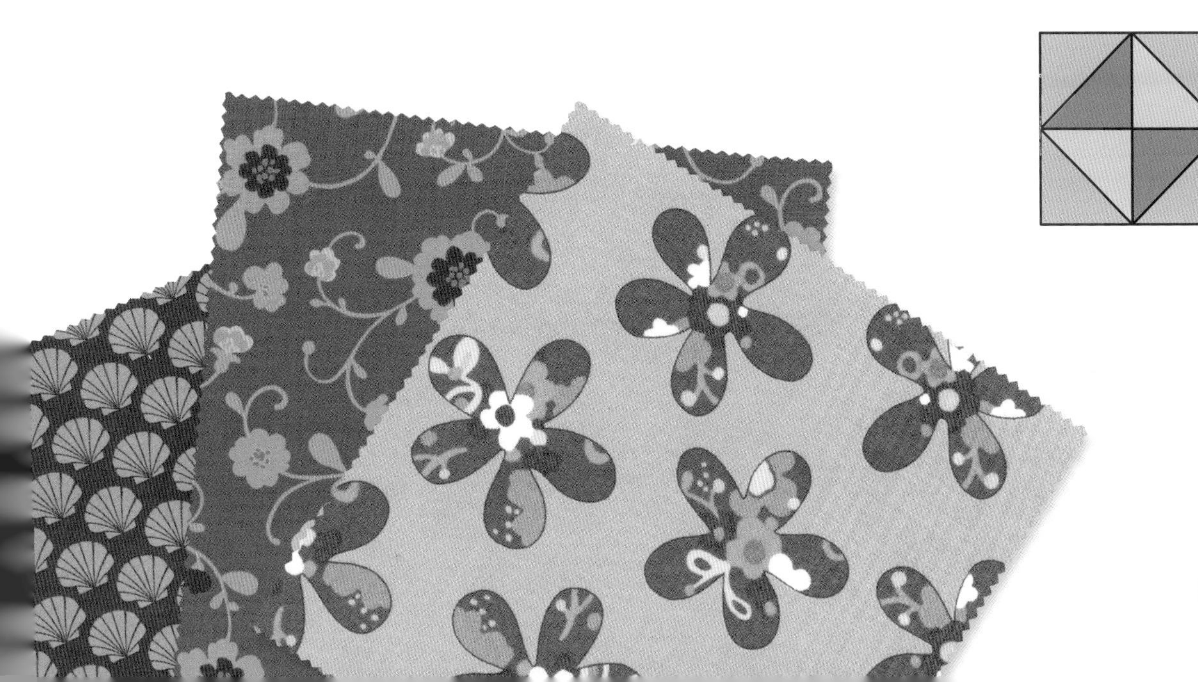

UNIT 1 (MAKE 24)

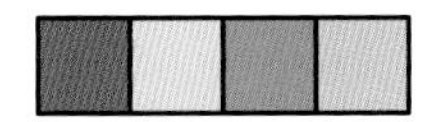

UNIT 2 (MAKE 24)

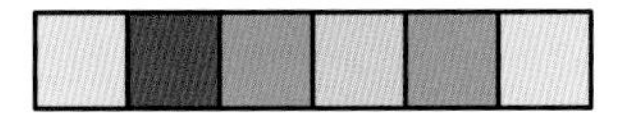

BLOCK (MAKE 12)

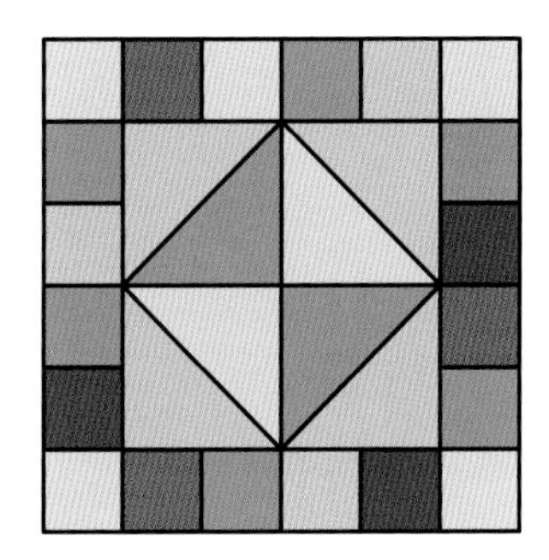

ROW (MAKE 4)

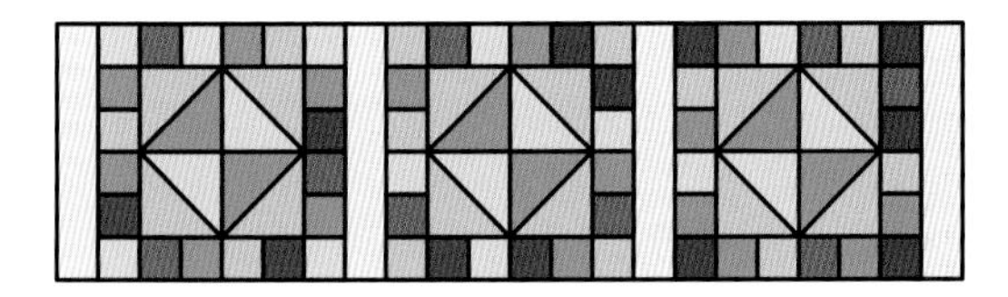

SASHING ROW (MAKE 5)

SIDE BORDER (MAKE 2)

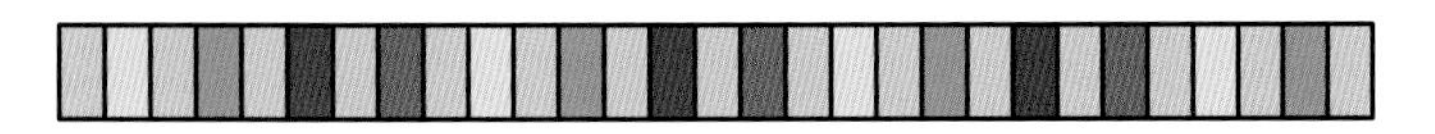

TOP/BOTTOM BORDER (MAKE 2)

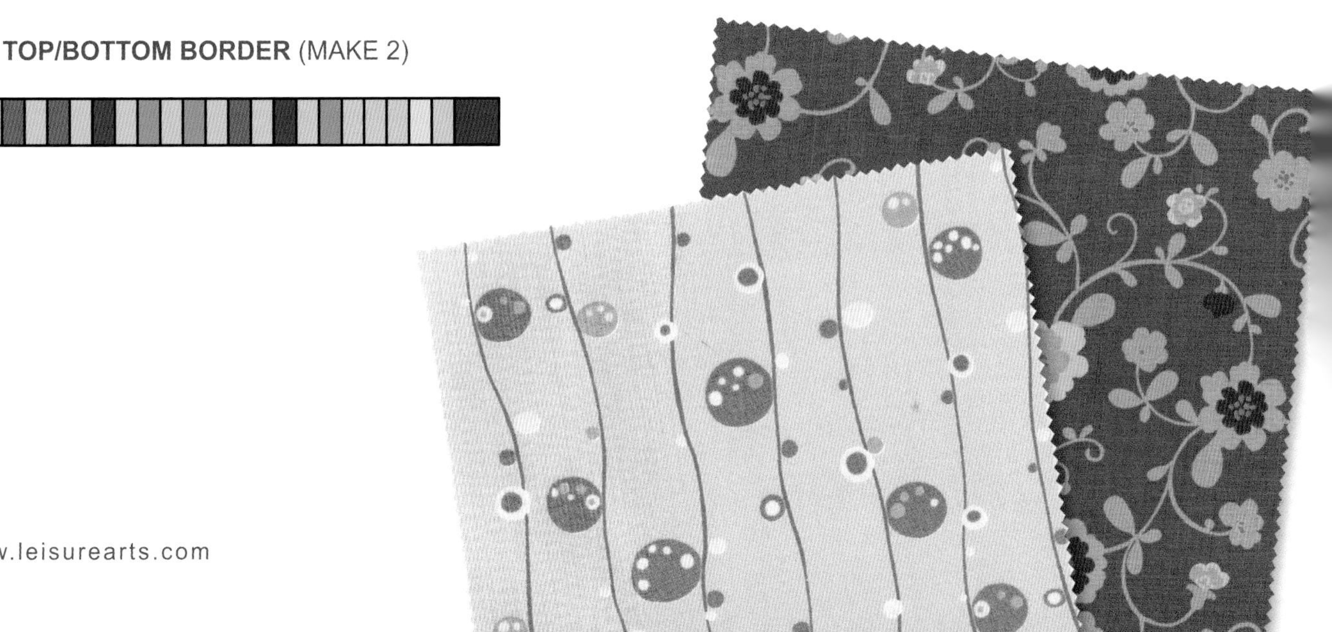

6. Sew 4 **small squares** together to make UNIT 1. Make 24 Unit 1's.
7. Sew 6 small squares together to make UNIT 2. Make 24 Unit 2's.
8. Sew 1 Unit 1 to opposite sides of 1 Block Center. Sew 1 Unit 2 to each remaining side of block center to make BLOCK. Make 12 Blocks.

assembling the quilt top center

Refer to QUILT TOP DIAGRAM *for placement.*

1. Sew 4 **sashings** and 3 Blocks together to make a ROW. Make 4 Rows.
2. Sew 3 sashings and 4 **sashing squares** together to make a SASHING ROW. Make 5 Sashing Rows.
3. Sew Rows and Sashing Rows together to make QUILT TOP CENTER.

adding the borders

1. Trim 4 red **border corner squares** to $4^1/_2$" x $4^1/_2$".
2. Matching long edges and alternating teal and assorted rectangles, sew 15 teal and 14 assorted **border rectangles** together to make SIDE BORDER. Make 2 Side Borders.
3. Matching long edges and alternating teal and assorted rectangles, sew 11 teal and 11 assorted **border rectangles** and 2 red **border corner quares** together to make TOP/BOTTOM BORDER. Make 2 Top/Bottom Borders.
4. Matching centers and corners, sew Side then Top/Bottom Borders to Quilt Top Center.

completing the quilt

1. Follow **Quilting**, page 74, to layer and quilt as desired. My quilt is machine quilted with scallop shells, palm trees, and mermaids in the block centers and a wave in the block borders. There are starfish in the sashings and scallop shells and bubbles in the outer border.
2. Refer to **Making A Hanging Sleeve**, page 75, to make and attach a hanging sleeve, if desired.
3. Use **binding strips** and follow **Making Double-Fold Binding**, page 76, to make **binding**. Follow **Attaching Binding**, page 76, to bind quilt.

Tip: For a really scrappy look, I cut my binding strips into assorted lengths ranging from 10" to 30" and included a few scrap pieces leftover from the blocks and border.

QUILT TOP DIAGRAM

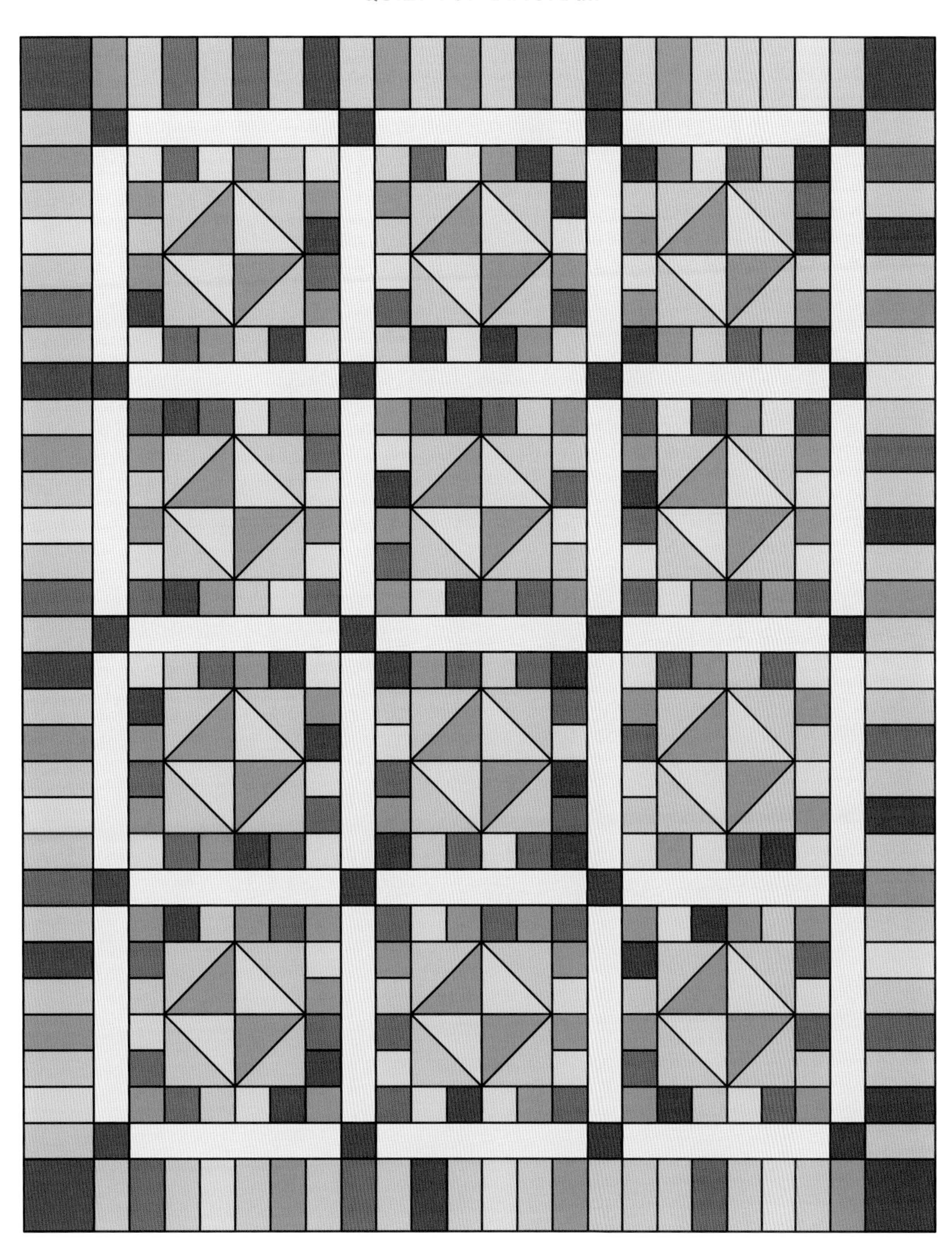

flirt

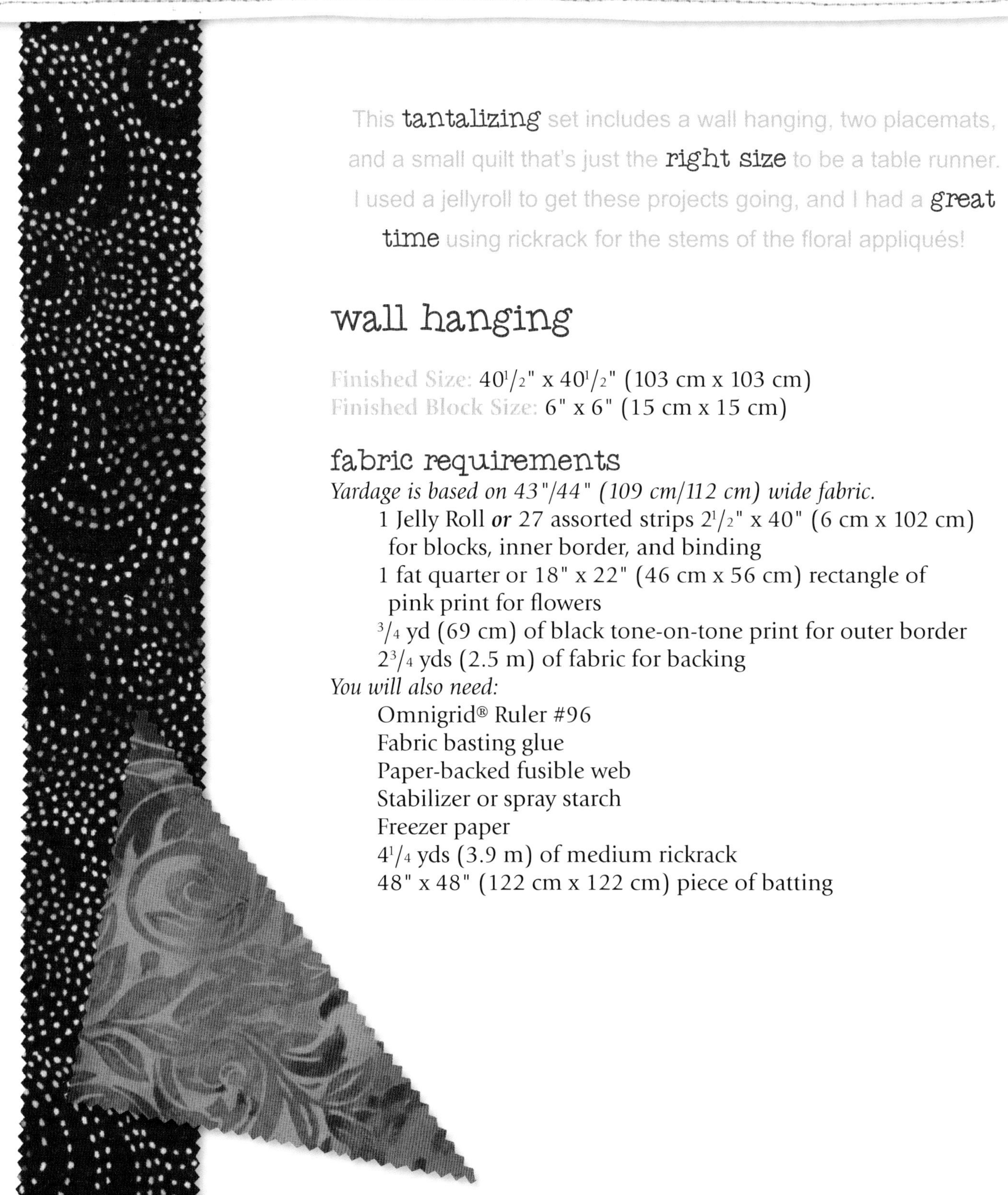

This **tantalizing** set includes a wall hanging, two placemats, and a small quilt that's just the **right size** to be a table runner. I used a jellyroll to get these projects going, and I had a **great time** using rickrack for the stems of the floral appliqués!

wall hanging

Finished Size: 40 1/2" x 40 1/2" (103 cm x 103 cm)
Finished Block Size: 6" x 6" (15 cm x 15 cm)

fabric requirements

Yardage is based on 43"/44" (109 cm/112 cm) wide fabric.

- 1 Jelly Roll ***or*** 27 assorted strips 2 1/2" x 40" (6 cm x 102 cm) for blocks, inner border, and binding
- 1 fat quarter or 18" x 22" (46 cm x 56 cm) rectangle of pink print for flowers
- 3/4 yd (69 cm) of black tone-on-tone print for outer border
- 2 3/4 yds (2.5 m) of fabric for backing

You will also need:

- Omnigrid® Ruler #96
- Fabric basting glue
- Paper-backed fusible web
- Stabilizer or spray starch
- Freezer paper
- 4 1/4 yds (3.9 m) of medium rickrack
- 48" x 48" (122 cm x 122 cm) piece of batting

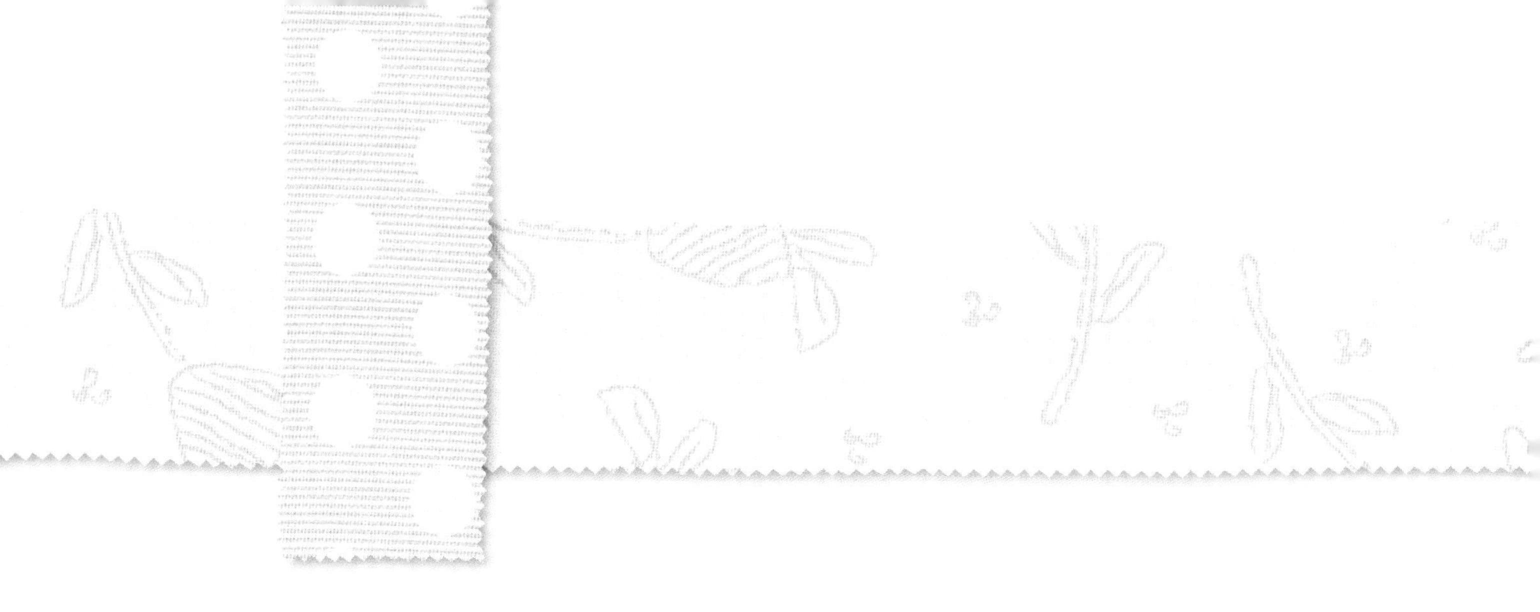

organizing the pre-cuts

My Jelly Roll only contained three basic colorways, creams, greens, and blacks. I divided the strips into lights (creams), mediums (greens), and darks (blacks). Go ahead and separate your strips into groups. This should be easy to do with almost any fabric line.

From light strips:

- Select 7 strips for blocks.

From medium strips:

- Select 4 strips for inner borders.
- Select 3 strips for blocks.
- Select 2 strips for setting triangles and corner triangles.
- Select 6 strips for binding.

From dark strips:

- Select 4 strips for blocks, small triangles and inner border corner squares.
- Select 1 strip for circles.

cutting the pieces

*Follow **Rotary Cutting**, page 70, to cut fabric. All measurements include 1/4" seam allowances. When instructed to cut **triangles**, use Omnigrid Ruler #96 and follow manufacturer's instructions for 2" **finished** triangles. Refer to **Preparing Fusible Appliqués**, page 72, to use petal and circle patterns, page 69.*

From light strips:

- Cut 69 **squares** 2 1/2" x 2 1/2".
- Cut 36 **triangles**.

From medium strips:

- Cut 4 **inner borders** 2 1/2" x 28 1/2".
- Cut 36 **squares** 2 1/2" x 2 1/2".
- Cut 24 **triangles**.
- Cut 6 **binding strips** 1 1/2" wide.

From dark strips:

- Cut 10 **squares** 2 1/2" x 2 1/2". Cut 2 of the squares in half once diagonally to make 4 **small triangles**.
- Cut 44 **triangles**.
- Cut 17 **circles**.

From pink print:

- Cut 51 **petals**.

From black tone-on-tone print:

- Cut 2 **side outer borders** 5 1/2" x 30".
- Cut 2 **top/bottom outer borders** 5 1/2" x 40".

making the blocks

*Follow **Piecing And Pressing**, page 71, to make the Blocks. Match right sides and use 1/4" seam allowances throughout. Refer to **Machine Appliqué**, page 72, for technique.*

nine-patch blocks

1. Sew 4 **light** like print **squares,** 4 **medium** like print **squares,** and 1 **dark square** together to make NINE-PATCH BLOCK. Make 4 Nine-Patch Blocks.

flower blocks

1. Matching long edges, sew 1 **light** and 1 **dark triangle** together to make TRIANGLE-SQUARE. Make 36 Triangle-Squares.
2. Sew 4 Triangle-Squares and 5 assorted **light squares** together to make BACKGROUND. Make 9 Backgrounds.
3. Cut 9 **stems**, each 3 1/2" long, from rickrack. Arrange 1 stem on each Background. Use basting glue to draw stem placement lines. Position stems over glue lines; allow to dry.
4. Arrange and fuse 3 **petals** and 1 **circle** to each Background. Straight stitch stems to Backgrounds. Machine Appliqué around petals and circles to make 9 FLOWER BLOCKS.

NINE-PATCH BLOCK (MAKE 4)

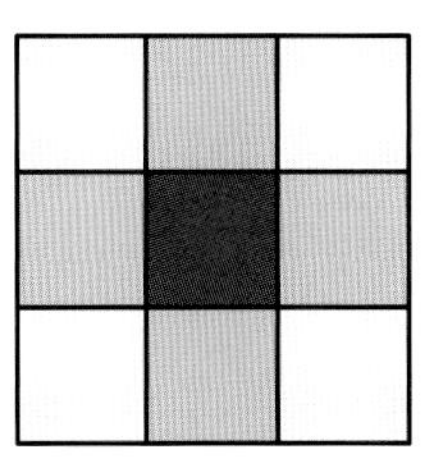

TRIANGLE-SQUARE (MAKE 36)

BACKGROUND (MAKE 9)

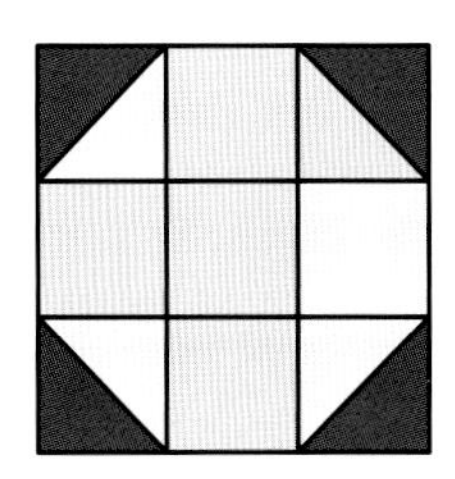

FLOWER BLOCK (MAKE 9)

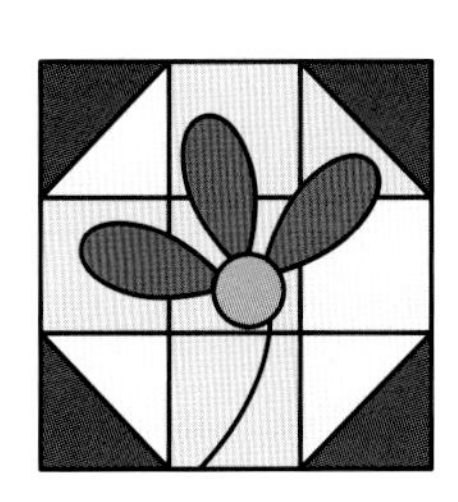

UNIT 1

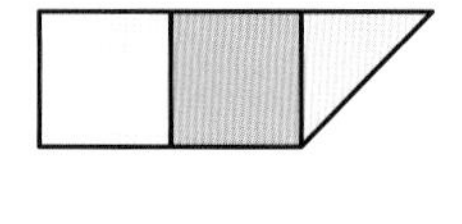

UNIT 2

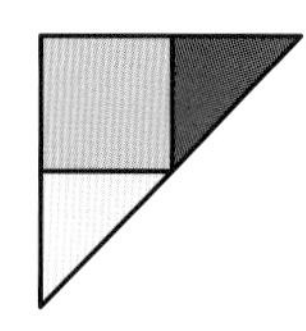

SETTING TRIANGLE (MAKE 8)

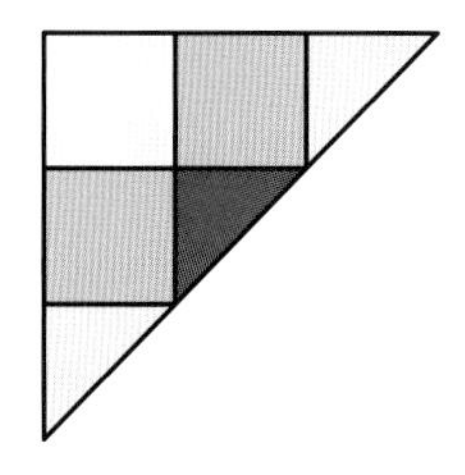

CORNER TRIANGLE (MAKE 4)

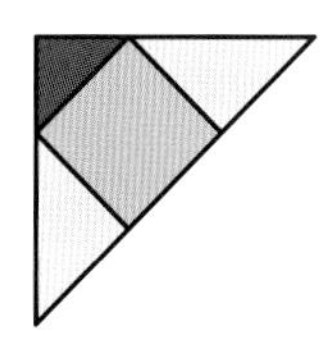

FIG. 1

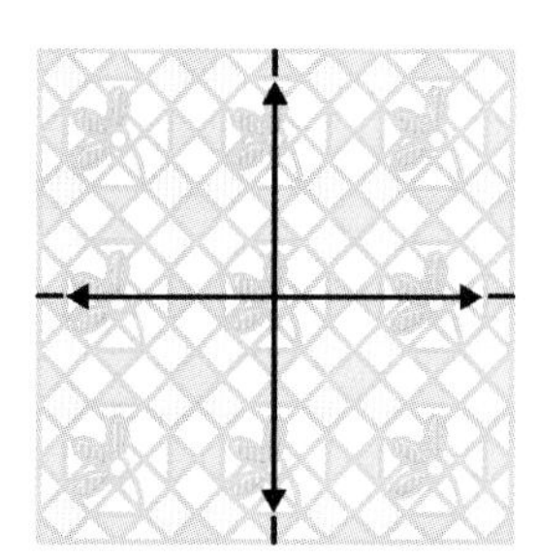

assembling the quilt top

Refer to QUILT TOP DIAGRAM for placement. ***Note:*** *Outer edges of Setting and Corner Triangles will be bias edges. Handle these edges carefully to avoid stretching or distorting. The dark small triangles are overcut and will be trimmed after assembling the Quilt Top Center.*

1. For setting triangles, sew 1 **light square, 1 medium square,** and **1 medium triangle** together to make UNIT 1.
2. Sew **1 medium square, dark triangle,** and **1 medium triangle** together to make UNIT 2.
3. Sew **Units 1** and **2** together to make SETTING TRIANGLE. Make 8 Setting Triangles.
4. For corner triangles, sew 1 **medium square, 2 medium triangles** and 1 **dark small triangle** together to make CORNER TRIANGLE. Make 4 Corner Triangles.
5. Referring to **Assembly Diagram**, sew **Corner Triangles**, **Setting Triangles**, and **Blocks** together to make QUILT TOP CENTER.
6. Keeping a $^1/_4$" seam allowance and a 90° angle at corners, square Quilt Top Center.

adding the borders

1. Cut four $28^1/_2$" lengths of rickrack. Use basting glue to draw a placement line down the center of each **inner border**. Position rickrack over glue lines; allow to dry. Straight stitch rickrack to inner borders.
2. Mark the center of each edge of the Quilt Top Center. Mark the center of each inner and **outer border**.
3. Measure through the center of the Quilt Top Center to determine length for inner borders (FIG. 1). Trim inner borders to this measurement.
4. Matching centers and corners, sew 1 inner border to opposite sides of Quilt Top Center. Sew 1 **dark square** to each end of remaining inner borders. Sew inner borders to top and bottom of Quilt Top Center.
5. Sew **side,** then **top/bottom outer borders** to Quilt Top Center.

completing the quilt

1. Follow **Quilting**, page 74, to layer and quilt as desired. My quilt is machine quilted with outline quilting around the appliqués. There are small circles in the Flower Blocks and swirls and leaves in the Nine-Patch Blocks. The flowers have a swirl in the center of each petal. The inner border has waves and there is a leaf and vine in the outer border.
2. With dull side facing out, match short edges and fold a 6" x 40" piece of freezer paper in half. Joining where indicated, trace border scallop, page 69, onto freezer paper. Cut out on drawn lines; unfold. With shiny side of paper facing down, align center of pattern with center of 1 outer border and angled edges of pattern with outer border corners; press pattern onto border. Trace around scallops. Repeat for each border. Trim border on drawn line.
3. Use **binding strips** and follow **Making Single-Fold Binding**, page 76, to make **binding**. Follow **Attaching Binding**, page 76, to bind quilt.
4. Center and fuse 3 **petals** and 1 **circle** in the center of each scallop. Machine Appliqué around petals and circles.

ASSEMBLY DIAGRAM

QUILT TOP DIAGRAM

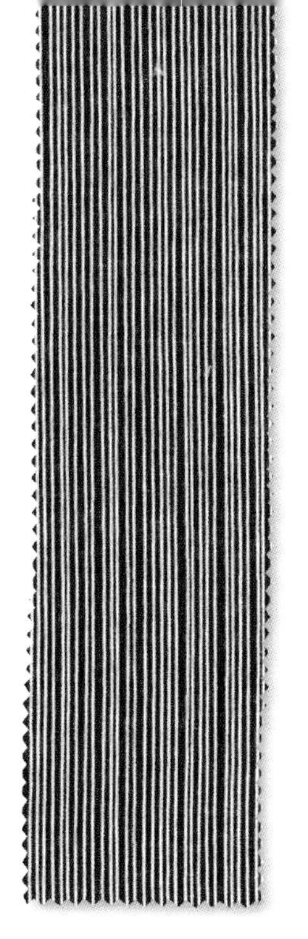

table topper

Finished Size:
29" x 23"
(74 cm x 58 cm)
Finished Block Size:
11" x 11"
(28 cm x 28 cm)

fabric requirements

Yardage is based on 43"/44" (109 cm/112 cm) wide fabric. The table topper is made using Jelly Roll strips leftover from the Wall Hanging.

24 light strips $2^1/_2$" x $6^3/_8$" (6 cm x 16 cm)
24 dark strips $2^1/_2$" x $6^3/_8$" (6 cm x 16 cm)
$^1/_8$ yd (11 cm) of pink print
$^1/_4$ yd (23 cm) of black polka dot print
$^1/_4$ yd (23 cm) of black tone-on-tone print for binding
$^7/_8$ yd (80 cm) of fabric for backing

You will also need:

Paper-backed fusible web
Stabilizer or spray starch
33" x 27" (84 cm x 69 cm) piece of batting

cutting the pieces

*Follow **Rotary Cutting**, page 70, to cut fabric. Cut all strips from the selvage-to-selvage width of the fabric. All measurements include 1/4" seam allowances. Refer to **Preparing Fusible Appliqués**, page 72, to use circle pattern, page 69.*

From pink print:

- Cut 2 **strips** 1 1/2" x 22 1/2".
- Cut 4 **circles**.

From black polka dot:

- Cut 2 **strips** 2 1/2" x 22 1/2".

From black tone-on-tone print:

- Cut 4 **binding strips** 1 1/2" wide.

making the blocks

*Follow **Piecing And Pressing**, page 71, to make the Blocks. Match right sides and use 1/4" seam allowances throughout. Refer to **Machine Appliqué**, page 72, for technique.*

1. Matching long edges, sew 3 **light strips** together to make UNIT 1. Trim 1/8" from 1 outer edge of 1 strip. Unit should measure 6 3/8" x 6 3/8". Make 8 Unit 1's.
2. Repeat Step 1 using 3 **dark strips** to make UNIT 2. Make 8 Unit 2's.
3. Draw a diagonal line on the wrong side of each Unit 1 (FIG. 1).
4. With right sides together, refer to FIG. 2 to place 1 Unit 1 (with trimmed strip at bottom) on top of 1 Unit 2 (with trimmed strip at right). Stitch 1/4" from each side of drawn line (FIG. 3).
5. Cut along drawn line and press seam allowance toward Unit 2 to make 2 TRIANGLE-SQUARES. Triangle-Square should measure 6" x 6". Make 16 Triangle-Squares.
6. Sew 4 Triangle-Squares together to make PINWHEEL BLOCK. Make 4 Pinwheel Blocks.
7. Fuse 1 circle to the center of each Pinwheel Block. Machine Appliqué around circles.

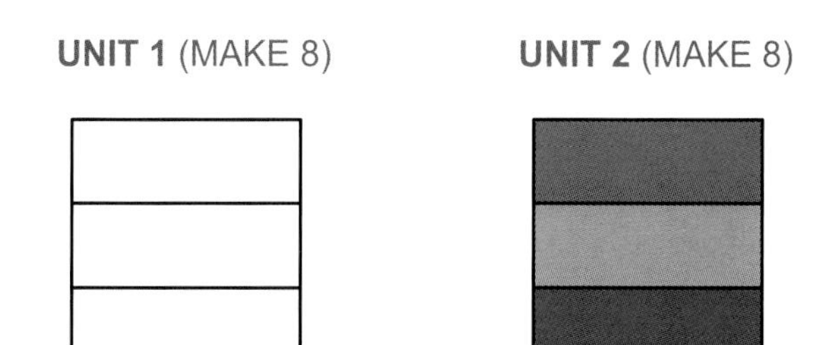

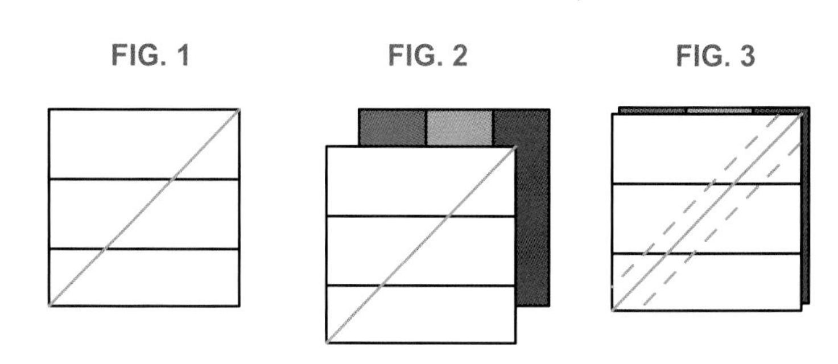

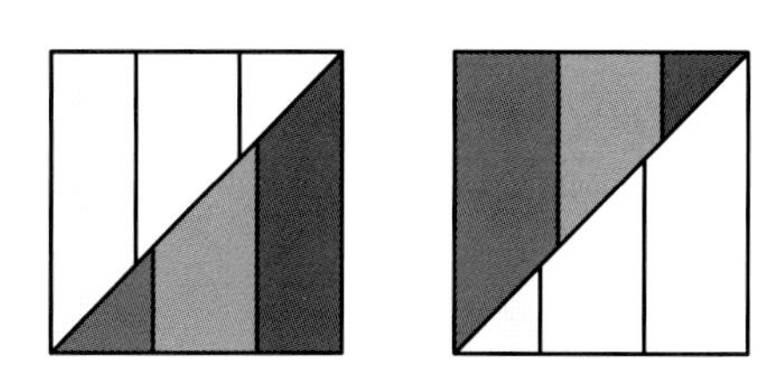

ROW (MAKE 2)

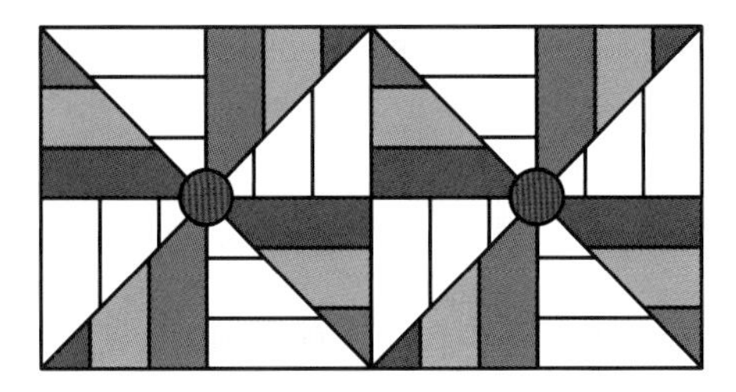

TABLE TOPPER DIAGRAM

assembling the tabble topper

Refer to TABLE TOPPER DIAGRAM *for placement.*

1. Sew 2 Pinwheel Blocks together to make ROW. Make 2 Rows.
2. Sew Rows together to make **Table Topper Center**.
3. Matching long edges, sew 1 pink print and 1 black polka dot strip together to make **Border**. Make 2 Borders.
4. Sew 1 Border to opposite sides of the Table Topper Center.

completing the table topper

1. Follow **Quilting**, page 74, to layer and quilt as desired. My table topper is machine quilted with large circles in the black polka dot strips, a wave in the pink inner border, and an all-over continuous swirl in the blocks. There is outline quilting around the circles.
2. Use **binding strips** and follow **Making Single-Fold Binding**, page 76, to make **binding**. Follow **Pat's Machine-Sewn Binding**, page 78, to bind table topper.

placemats

Finished Size: 19" x 14" (48 cm x 36 cm)

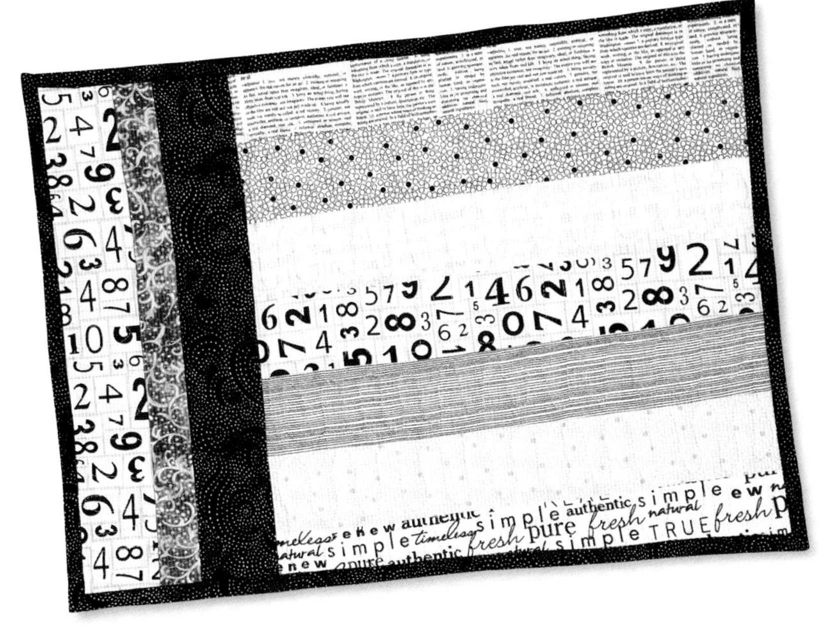

fabric requirements

Yardage is based on 43"/44" (109 cm/112 cm) wide fabric. The placemats are made using Jelly Roll strips leftover from the Wall Hanging. Fabric requirements are for 2 placemats.

16 light strips 2 1/2" x 13 1/2" (6 cm x 34 cm)
1/8 yd (11 cm) of pink print
1/4 yd (23 cm) of black tone-on-tone print (includes binding)
1/2 yd (46 cm) of fabric for backing

You will also need:

Two 23" x 18" (58 cm x 46 cm) pieces of batting

cutting the pieces

*Follow **Rotary Cutting**, page 70, to cut fabric. Cut all strips from the selvage-to-selvage width of the fabric. All measurements include 1/4" seam allowances.*

From pink print:

- Cut 2 **strips** 1 1/2" x 13 1/2".

From black tone-on-tone print:

- Cut 2 **strips** 2 1/2" x 13 1/2".
- Cut 4 **binding strips** 1 1/2" wide.

making the placemats

1. Matching long edges, sew 7 light strips together to make UNIT 1. Make 2 Unit 1's. Angling ruler as desired, trim Unit 1 to 13 1/2" x 13 1/2" to make UNIT 2. Make 2 Unit 2's.
2. Matching long edges, sew 1 black tone-on-tone print, 1 pink print, and 1 light **strip** together to make UNIT 3. Make 2 Unit 3's.
3. Referring to PLACEMAT TOP DIAGRAM, sew Units 2 and 3 together to make PLACEMAT TOP. Make 2 Placemat Tops.

UNIT 1 (MAKE 2)

UNIT 2 (MAKE 2)

UNIT 3 (MAKE 2)

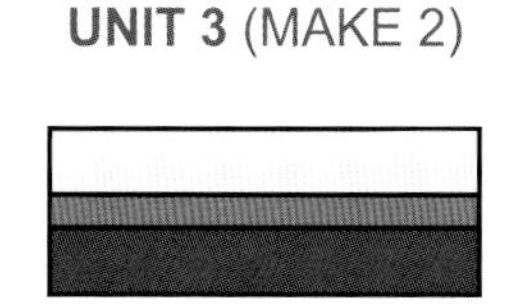

PLACEMAT TOP (MAKE 2)

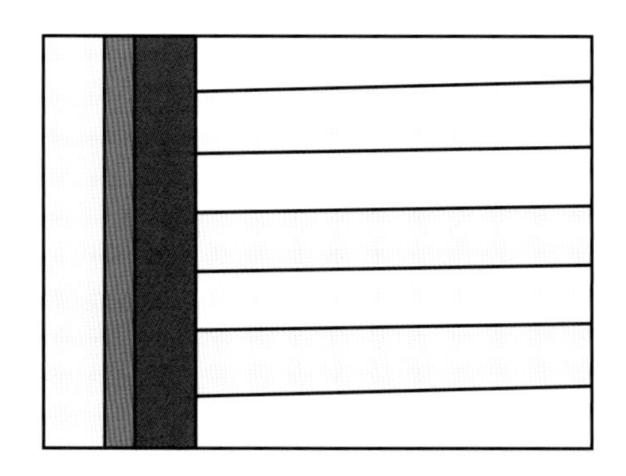

completing the placemats

1. Follow **Quilting**, page 74, to layer and quilt as desired. My Placemats are machine quilted with a wave pattern in each strip. There is outline quilting along the long edges of the black tone-on tone strip.
2. Use **binding strips** and follow **Making Single-Fold Binding**, page 76, to make **binding**. Follow **Pat's Machine-Sewn Binding**, page 78, to bind Placemats.

choose your SNOOZE

Love **red and white** together? Me, too! It's such a **classic color combination** that you can almost always find the **perfect** pre-cuts to make pillows like these. Why three pillows? I couldn't stop at one!

checkerboard pillow

Finished Size: 14" x 14" (36 cm x 36 cm)

fabric requirements

Yardage is based on 43"/44" (109 cm/112 cm) wide fabric with a usable width of 42" (107 cm). Two Honey Buns will make all three pillows.

7 assorted red print strips 1¹/₂" x 22" (4 cm x 56 cm)
7 assorted white print strips 1¹/₂" x 22" (4 cm x 56 cm)
³/₈ yd (34 cm) of red print for pillow back

You will also need:

14" x 14" (36 cm x 36 cm) pillow form

cutting the pieces

Follow ***Rotary Cutting****, page 70, to cut fabric. All measurements include ¹/₄" seam allowances.*

From red print:

- Cut 2 **pillow backs** 11³/₄" x 14¹/₂".

making the pillow top

Refer to Assembly Diagram and follow ***Piecing And Pressing****, page 71, to make the pillow top. Match right sides and use $\frac{1}{4}$" seam allowances throughout.*

1. Matching long edges, sew 1 white print and 1 red print **strip** together to make STRIP SET A. Cut across Strip Set A at $1\frac{1}{2}$" intervals to make UNIT 1. Make 14 Unit 1's.
2. Matching long edges and alternating colors, sew 7 Unit 1's together to make a vertical ROW 1. Make 2 Row 1's.
3. Repeat Steps 1 and 2 to make 2 of each Row 2-7 for a total of 14 Rows.
4. Sew Rows together to make **Pillow Top**.

completing the pillow

1. Press 1 long edge of each **pillow back** $\frac{1}{4}$" to the wrong side twice. Topstitch hem close to the folded edges.
2. With right sides facing up, overlap the two hemmed edges of the pillow backs until the overall measurement is $14\frac{1}{2}$" x $14\frac{1}{2}$". Baste the overlapped edges together.
3. Matching right sides, sew the Pillow Top and back together; clip corners.
4. Turn pillow right side out, press, and insert pillow form.

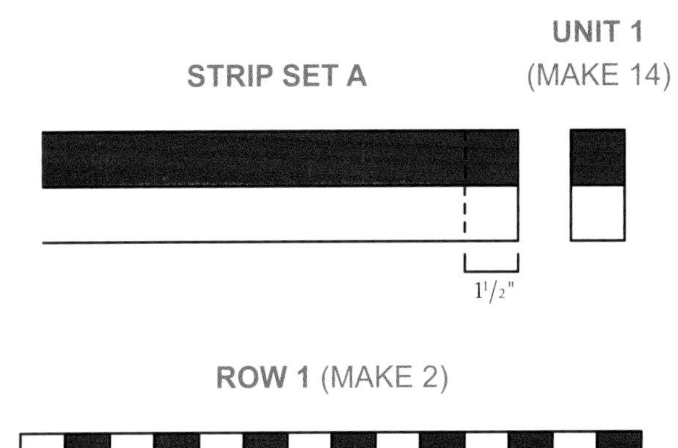

ASSEMBLY DIAGRAM

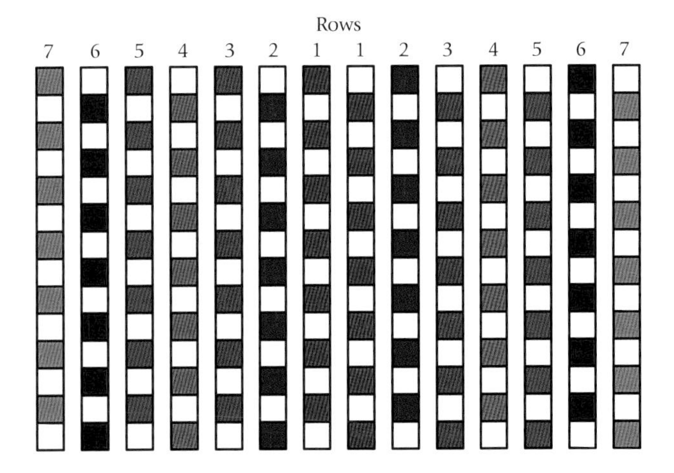

PILLOW TOP DIAGRAM

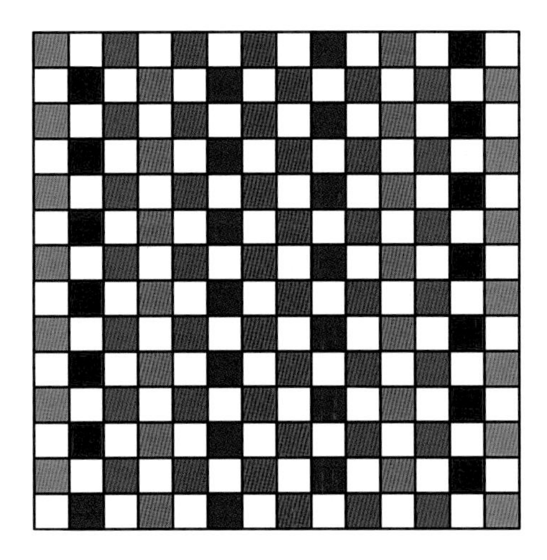

fun with rectangles pillow

Finished Size: 17½" x 18" (44 cm x 46 cm)
Finished Block Size: 4½" x 9" (11 cm x 23 cm)

fabric requirements

*Yardage is based on 43"/44" (109 cm/112 cm) wide fabric with a usable width of 42" (107 cm). **Note**: For the white strips, I used 2 strips each of 7 fabrics.*

14 white print strips 1½" x 42" (4 cm x 107 cm)
6 red print strips 1½" x 42" (4 cm x 107 cm)
2 red print strips 1½" x 42" (4 cm x 107 cm) for side borders
½ yd (46 cm) of red print for pillow back

You will also need:

18" x 18" (46 cm x 46 cm) pillow form

cutting the pieces

*Follow **Rotary Cutting**, page 70, to cut fabric. All measurements include ¼" seam allowances.*

From white print strips:
- Cut 14 **strips** 1½" x 26".

From red print strips:
- Cut 18 **strips** 1½" x 13".

From red print strips for border:
- Cut 4 **side border strips** 1½" x 18½".

From red print:
- Cut 2 **pillow backs** 13¼" x 18½".

making the blocks

*Follow **Piecing And Pressing**, page 71, to make the pillow top. Match right sides and use ¼" seam allowances throughout.*

1. Matching long edges, sew 14 assorted white **strips** together to make STRIP SET A. Cut across Strip Set A at 4" intervals to make UNIT 1. Make 6 Unit 1's.
2. Matching long edges, sew 6 assorted red **strips** together to make STRIP SET B. Make 3 Strip Set B's. Cut across each Strip Set B at 5½" intervals to make 2 UNIT 2's. Make 6 Unit 2's.

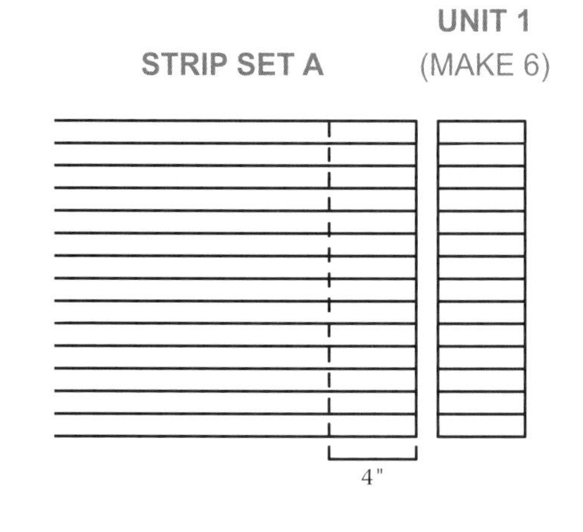

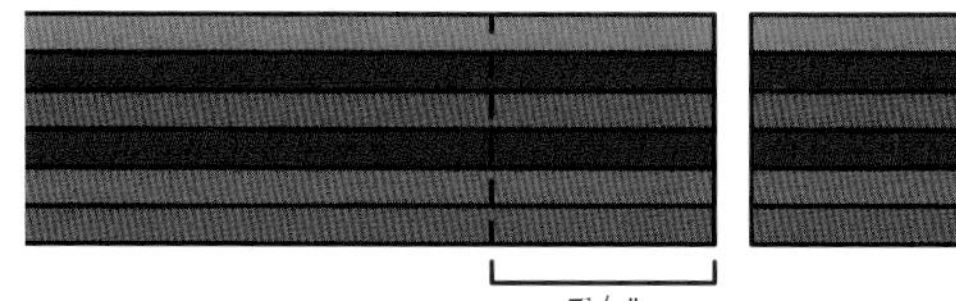
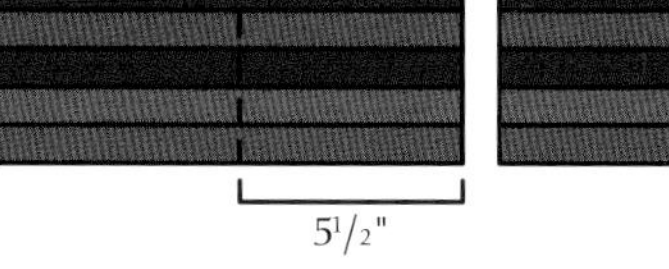

UNIT 3 (MAKE 12)

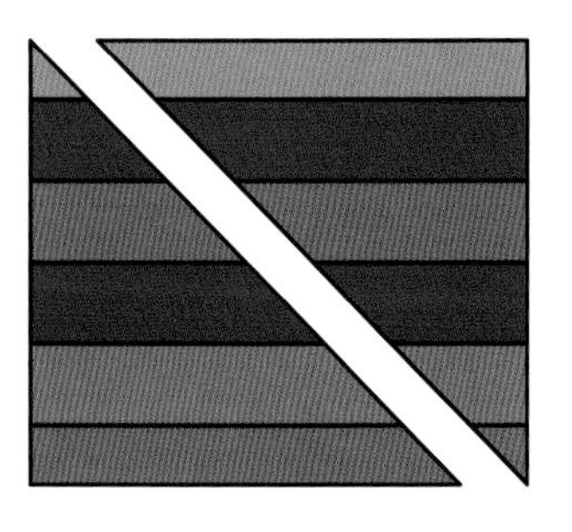

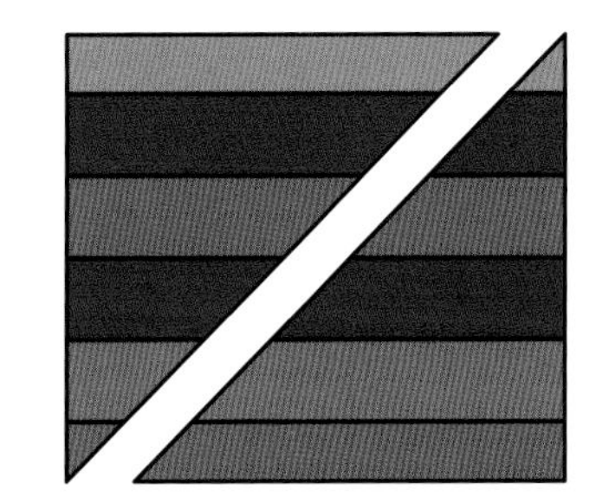

FIG. 1

FIG. 2

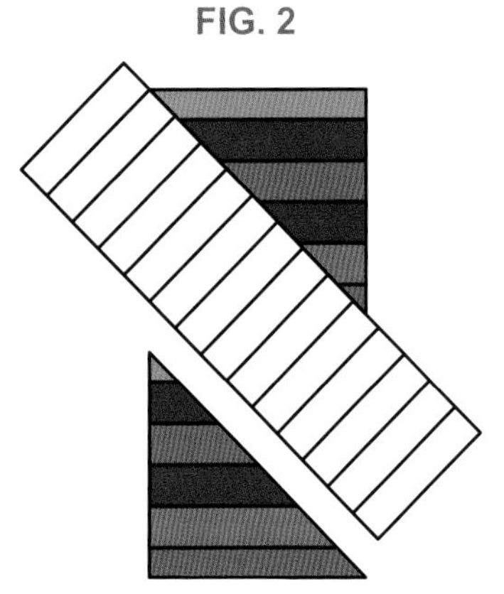

FIG. 3

FIG. 4

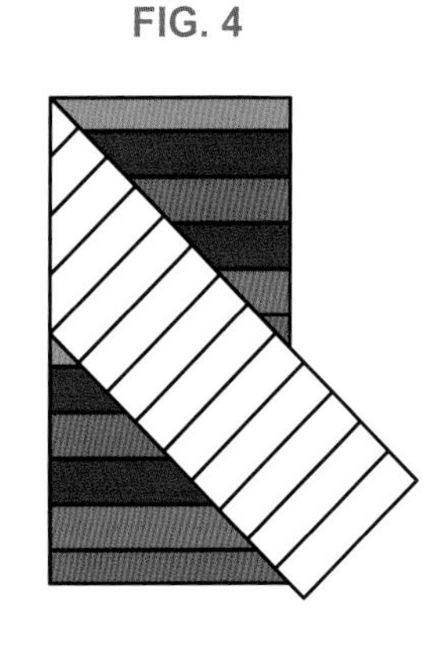

FIG. 5

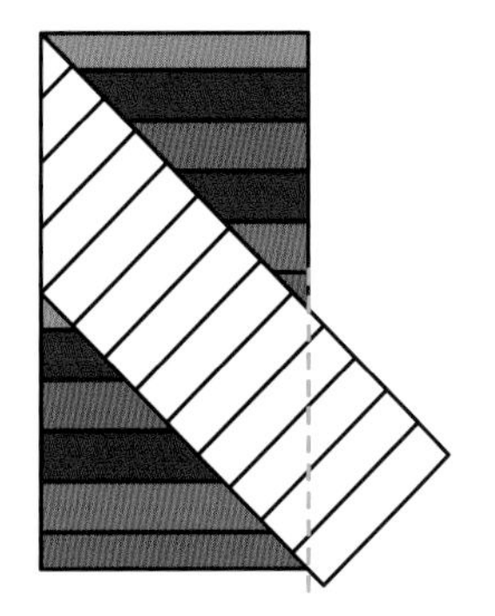

3. Trimming as desired from top and/or bottom strips, square each Unit 2 to $5\frac{1}{2}$" x $5\frac{1}{2}$". Cut each Unit 2 once diagonally to make 2 UNIT 3's. **Note:** For variety, I cut some of the Units from top left to bottom right and some from top right to bottom left. Make 12 Unit 3's.
4. Position 1 Unit 1 and 2 Unit 3's as shown (FIG. 1). **Note:** When I make the blocks, my placement is always freeform. After positioning the Unit 3's, I move Unit 1 diagonally to give me lots of variation between blocks.
5. Sew 1 Unit 3 to the top edge of Unit 1; open and press (FIG. 2).
6. Aligning edge of ruler with the outer edge of Unit 3, trim the excess portion of Unit 1 (FIG. 3).
7. Align the top left point of the remaining Unit 3 with the trimmed edge of Unit 1 (FIG. 4).
8. Sew Unit 3 to the bottom edge of Unit 1; open and press. Refer to Step 6 to trim the remaining excess portion of Unit 1 (FIG. 5).
9. Square BLOCK to 5" x $9\frac{1}{2}$". Make 6 Blocks.

BLOCK (MAKE 6)

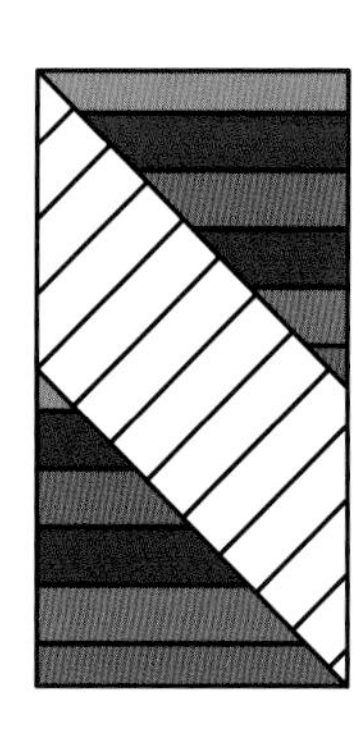

assembling the pillow top

Refer to PILLOW TOP DIAGRAM for placement.

1. Matching long edges, sew 3 Blocks together to make a ROW. Make 2 Rows.
2. Sew the Rows together to make **Pillow Top Center.**
3. Matching long edges, sew 2 **side border strips** together to make **Side Border**. Make 2 Side Borders.
4. Matching centers and corners, sew Side Borders to Pillow Top Center.

ROW (MAKE 2)

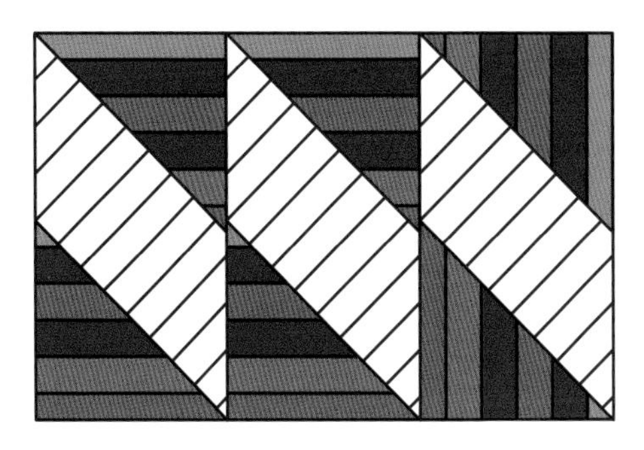

completing the pillow

1. Press 1 long edge of each **pillow back** $^1/_4$" to the wrong side twice. Topstitch hem close to the folded edges.
2. With right sides facing up, overlap the two hemmed edges of the pillow backs until the overall measurement is 18" x 18$^1/_2$". Baste the overlapped edges together.
3. Matching right sides, sew the Pillow Top and back together; clip corners.
4. Turn pillow right side out, press, and insert pillow form.

PILLOW TOP DIAGRAM

pinwheels pillow

Finished Size: 24" x 18"
(61 cm x 46 cm)
Finished Block Size: 9" x 9"
(23 cm x 23 cm)

fabric requirements

Yardage is based on 43"/44" (109 cm/112 cm) wide fabric with a usable width of 42" (107 cm).

11 red strips 1 1/2" x 42" (4 cm x 107 cm)
12 white strips 1 1/2" x 42" (4 cm x 107 cm)
5/8 yd (57 cm) of white print for pillow back
3/4 yd (69 cm) of white solid for pillow top backing

You will also need:

28" x 22" (71 cm x 56 cm) piece of batting
24" x 18" (61 cm x 46 cm) pillow form

organizing the pre-cuts

- Select 10 red strips for Triangle-Squares.
- Select 1 red strip for side borders.
- Select 10 white strips for Triangle-Squares.
- Select 2 white strips for side borders.

cutting the pieces

*Follow **Rotary Cutting**, page 70, to cut fabric. All measurements include 1/4" seam allowances.*

From white print:

- Cut 2 **pillow backs** 16 3/4" x 18 1/2".

From white solid:

- Cut 1 **pillow top backing** 28" x 22".

making the pillow top

*Follow **Piecing And Pressing**, page 71, to make the pillow top. Match right sides and use 1/4" seam allowances throughout.*

1. Matching long edges, sew 5 assorted red **strips** for Triangle-Squares together to make STRIP SET A. Make 2 Strip Set A's. Cut across Strip Set A's at 5 3/8" intervals to make UNIT 1's. Trim 1/8" from 1 outer edge of 1 strip. Unit 1 should measure 5 3/8" x 5 3/8". Make 8 Unit 1's.
2. Repeat Step 1 using white **strips** to make 8 UNIT 2's.

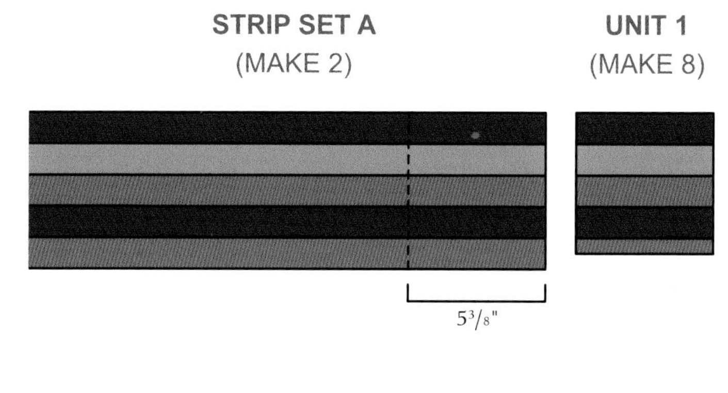

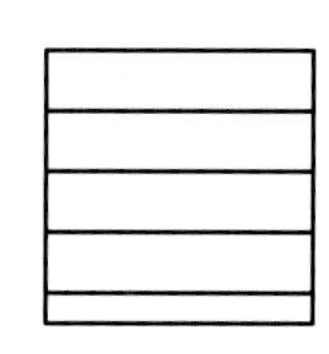

3. Draw a diagonal line on the wrong side of each Unit 2 (FIG. 1).
4. With right sides together, refer to FIG. 2 to place 1 Unit 1 (with trimmed strip at top) on top of 1 Unit 2 (with trimmed strip at right). Stitch $^1/_4$" from each side of drawn line (FIG. 3).
5. Cut along drawn line and press seam allowance toward Unit 2 to make 2 TRIANGLE-SQUARES. Make 16 Triangle-Squares.
6. Sew 4 Triangle-Squares together to make PINWHEEL BLOCK. Make 4 Pinwheel Blocks.
7. Sew Pinwheel Blocks together to make PILLOW TOP CENTER.
8. Matching long edges, sew 1 red and 2 white strips for borders together to make STRIP SET C. From Strip Set C, cut 2 SIDE BORDERS $18^1/_2$" x $3^1/_2$".
9. Sew one Side Border to opposite sides of Pillow Top Center to make **Pillow Top**.

completing the pillow

1. Follow **Quilting**, page 74, to layer and quilt the **pillow top backing**, batting, and pillow top. My Pillow Top is machine quilted with swirls in the red triangles and waves in the white triangles. There is outline quilting in the white border strips and waves in the red strips.
2. Press 1 long edge of each pillow back $^1/_4$" to the wrong side twice. Topstitch hem close to the folded edges.
3. With right sides facing up, overlap the two hemmed edges of the pillow backs until the overall measurement is $24^1/_2$" x $18^1/_2$". Baste the overlapped edges together.
4. Matching right sides, sew the Pillow Top and back together; clip corners.
5. Turn pillow right side out, press, and insert pillow form.

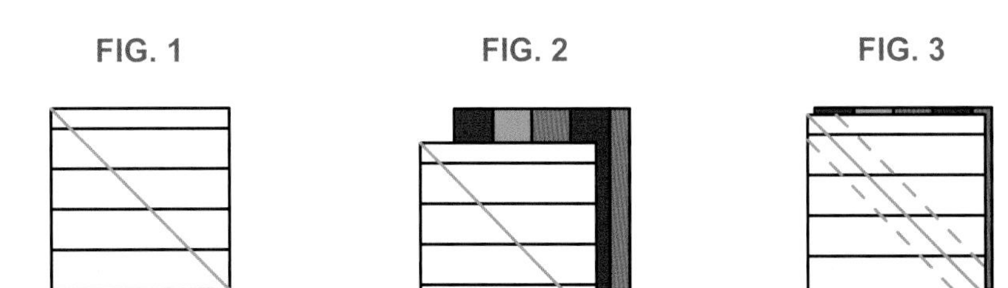

TRIANGLE-SQUARE (MAKE 16)

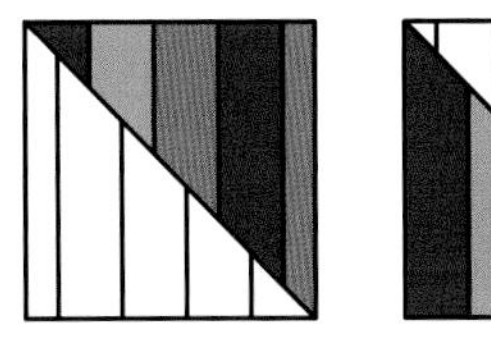
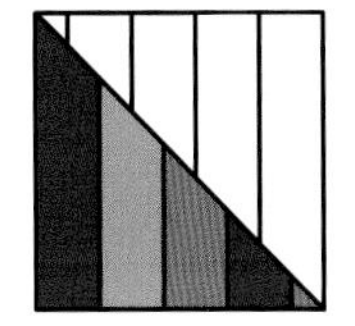

PINWHEEL BLOCK (MAKE 4)

STRIP SET C

SIDE BORDER (MAKE 2)

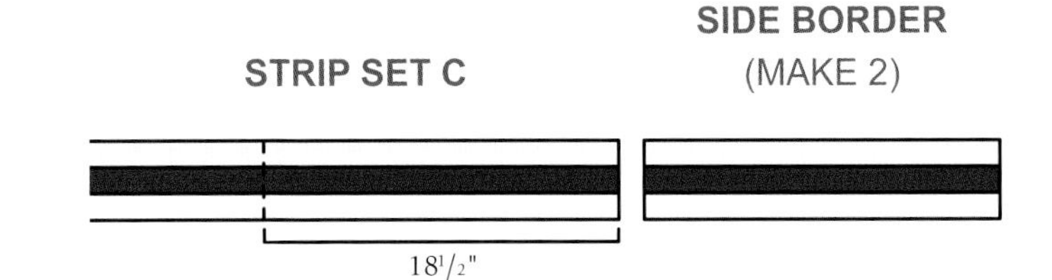

PILLOW TOP

under the sea

This ocean-themed fabric, with all its seaside hues, just begged to have a white-on-white setting. The blocks simply could not be easier, and they're such a quick and fun way to use honey bun and charm pack pre-cuts.

Finished Size: 43½" x 54⅛" (110 cm x 137 cm)
Finished Block Size: 7½" x 7½" (19 cm x 19 cm)

fabric requirements

Yardage is based on 43"/44" (109 cm/112 cm) wide fabric.

1 Honey Bun ***or*** 40 assorted strips 1½" x 40" (4 cm x 102 cm)
1 Charm Pack ***or*** 32 assorted squares 5" x 5" (13 cm x 13 cm)
1½ yds (1.4 m) of white tone-on-tone print
½ yd (46 cm) of green print for binding
3½ yds (3.2 m) of fabric for backing

You will also need:

51½" x 62⅛" (131 cm x 158 cm) piece of batting

organizing the pre-cuts

From Honey Bun *or* assorted strips:

- Separate the **strips** into lights and darks.

From Charm Packs or assorted squares:

- Select 20 assorted squares for the Log Cabin Block **centers**.
- Select 12 assorted squares for the Floating Square Block **centers**.

cutting the pieces

*Follow **Rotary Cutting**, page 70, to cut fabric. Cut all strips from the selvage-to-selvage width of the fabric. All measurements include 1/4" seam allowances.*

From white tone-on-tone print:

- Cut 8 strips 2" wide. From these strips, cut 24 **small rectangles** 2" x 5" and 24 **large rectangles** 2" x 8".
- Cut 2 strips 11 7/8" wide. From these strips, cut 4 squares 11 7/8" x 11 7/8". Cut each square twice diagonally to make 16 **setting triangles** (will use 14).
- Cut 1 strip 6 1/4" wide. From this strip, cut 2 squares 6 1/4" x 6 1/4". Cut each square once diagonally to make 4 **corner triangles**.

From green print:

- Cut 6 **binding strips** 2 1/2" wide.

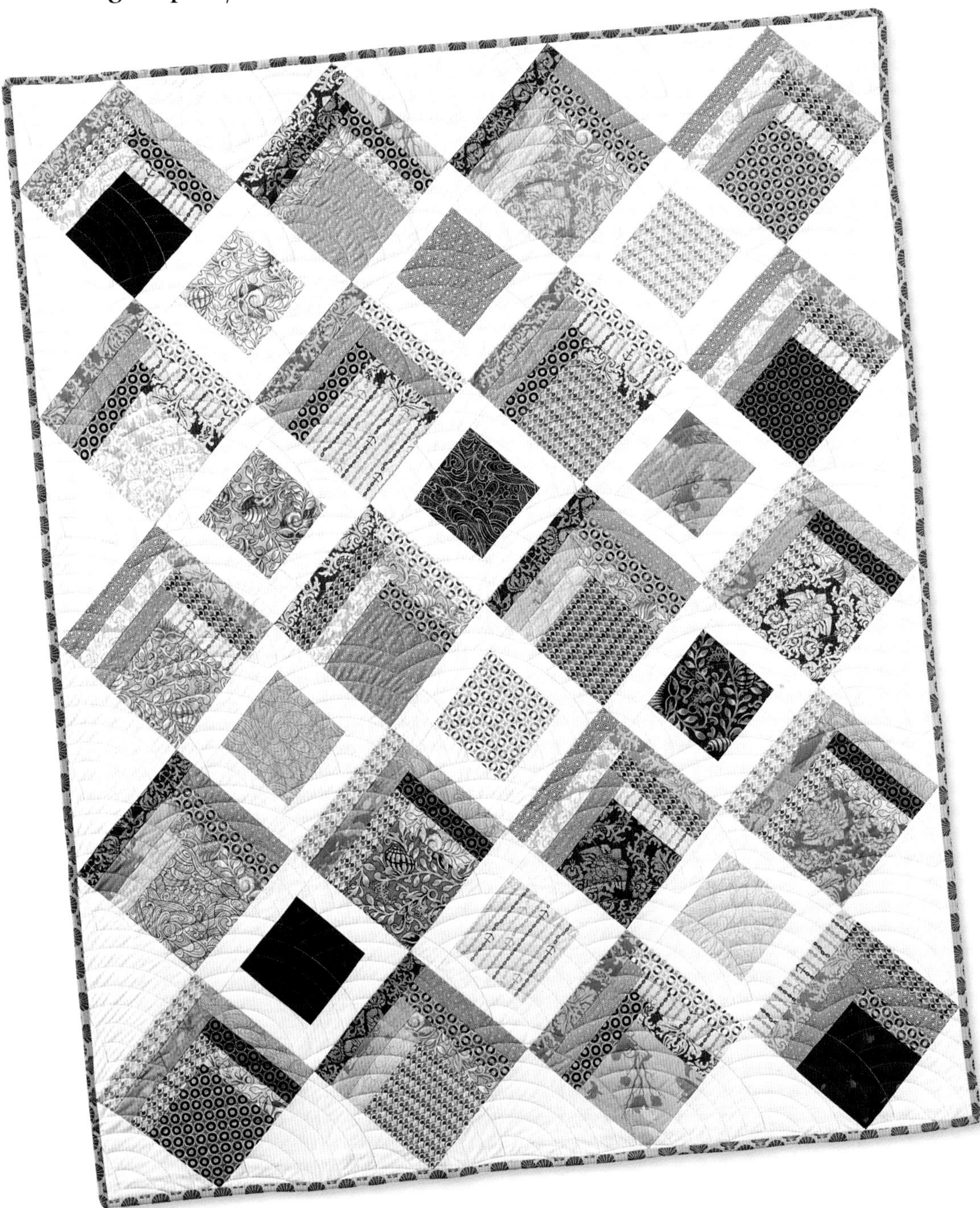

making the blocks

*Follow **Piecing And Pressing**, page 71, to make the Blocks. Match right sides and use $^{1}/_{4}$" seam allowances throughout. **Note:** When using dark center squares, choose light strips for logs 1 and 2. When using light center squares, choose dark strips for logs 1 and 2.*

log cabin block

1. Matching right sides and raw edges, place a **strip** for log 1 on 1 **center;** stitch (FIG. 1). Trim strip even with center (FIG. 2); press open (FIG. 3).
2. Turn center a $^{1}/_{4}$ turn to the right. Using the strip for log 2, repeat Step 1 (FIG. 4).
3. Turn center a $^{1}/_{4}$ turn back to the left (the original starting position). Using a different strip, repeat Step 1 to add log 3 (FIG. 5).
4. Continue adding logs in the same manner until there are 3 logs on each of the 2 sides of the center to make **Log Cabin Block.** Make 20 Log Cabin Blocks.

floating square block

1. Sew 1 **small rectangle** to opposite sides of 1 center (FIG. 6).
2. Sew 1 **large rectangle** to each remaining side of the center to make FLOATING SQUARE BLOCK. Make 12 Floating Square Blocks.

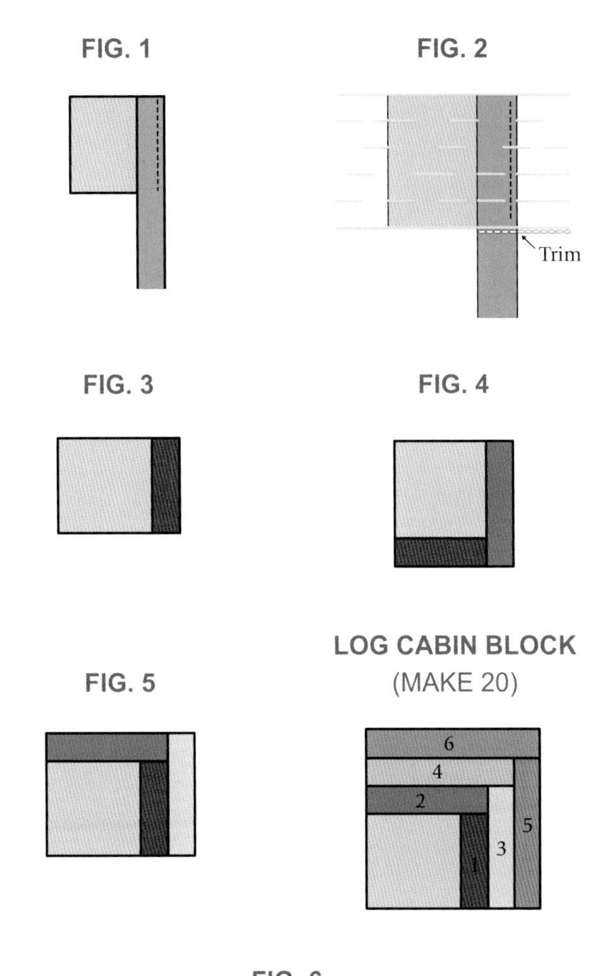

FIG. 6

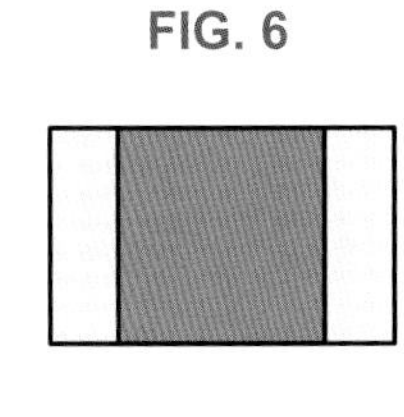

FLOATING SQUARE BLOCK
(MAKE 12)

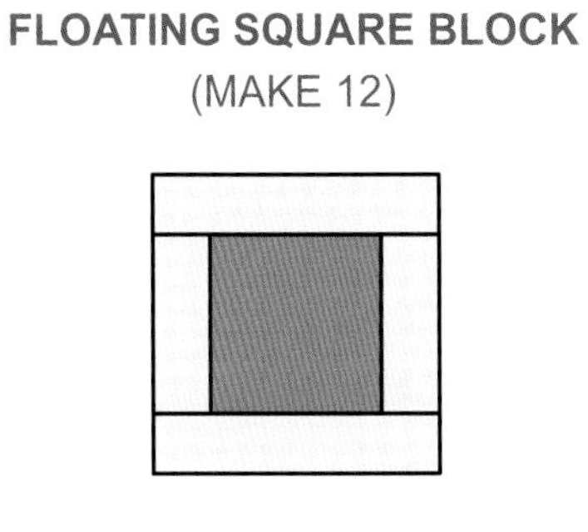

ASSEMBLY DIAGRAM

assembling the quilt top

1. Referring to the ASSEMBLY DIAGRAM, sew blocks and **setting triangles** together in diagonal rows to make QUILT TOP.
2. Sew 1 **corner triangle** to each corner of the Quilt Top.
3. Keeping a 90° angle at corners and allowing a $^1/_4$" seam allowance, square quilt by trimming outer edges of setting and corner triangles.

completing the quilt

1. Follow **Quilting**, page 74, to layer and quilt as desired. My quilt is machine quilted with an all-over Baptist Fan pattern.
2. Refer to **Making A Hanging Sleeve**, page 75, to make and attach a hanging sleeve, if desired.
3. Use **binding strips** and follow Making **Double-Fold Binding**, page 76, to make **binding**. Follow **Attaching Binding**, page 76, to bind quilt.

under the sea pillow

This quick and easy pillow is made using strips and partial strips leftover from the quilt.

Finished Size: 14" x 14" (36 cm x 36 cm)

fabric requirements

Yardage is based on 43"/44" (109 cm/112 cm) wide fabric with a usable width of 42". The term "strip" is used to indicate partial Honey Bun strips.

Assorted $1^1/_2$" (4 cm) wide **light print strips** [include some white tone-on-tone strips, trimmed to $1^1/_2$" (4 cm) wide] which, when added together short end to short end, total at least 150" (381 cm)

Assorted $1^1/_2$" (4 cm) wide **dark print strips** which, when added together short end to short end, total at least 150" (381 cm)

$^3/_8$ yd (34 cm) of fabric for pillow back

You will also need:

14" x 14" (36 cm x 36 cm) pillow form

cutting the pieces

*Follow **Rotary Cutting**, page 70, to cut fabric. All measurements include $^1/_4$" seam allowances.*

From backing fabric:

- Cut 2 **pillow backs** $11^3/_4$" x $14^1/_2$".

making the pillow top

*Follow **Piecing And Pressing**, page 71, to make the pillow top. Match right sides and use $^1/_4$" seam allowances throughout.*

1. Choosing strips of similar length, match long edges and pair 2 **strips** together. **Note:** For lots of variety, use short strips and really mix up the colors!
2. Sew each pair of strips together to make STRIP SET A's. Make a total of at least 150" of Strip Set A's.
3. Cut across Strip Set A's at $1^1/_2$" intervals to make UNIT 1's. Make 98 Unit 1's.
4. Matching short edges, sew 7 Unit 1's together to make a ROW. Make 14 Rows.
5. Matching long edges, sew Rows together to make **Pillow Top**.

completing the pillow

1. Press 1 long edge of each **pillow back** $^1/_4$" to the wrong side twice. Topstitch hem close to the folded edges.
2. With right sides facing up, overlap the two hemmed edges of the pillow backs until the overall measurement is $14^1/_2$" x $14^1/_2$". Baste the overlapped edges together.
3. Matching right sides, sew the Pillow Top and back together; clip corners.
4. Turn pillow right side out, press, and insert pillow form.

STRIP SET A

UNIT 1 (MAKE 98)

$1^1/_2$"

ROW (MAKE 14)

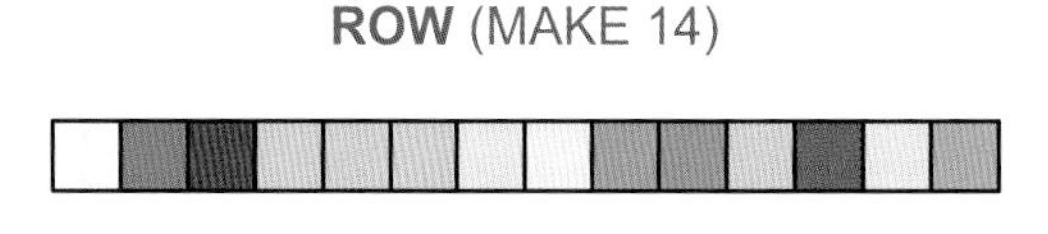

PILLOW TOP DIAGRAM

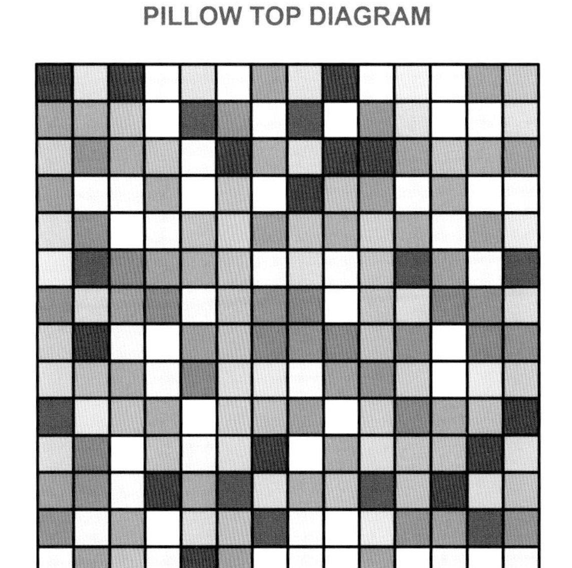

pretty PLATES

Did your grandmother have a Dresden Plate quilt in her collection? It's one of those traditional quilt patterns that bring to mind colorful jars of home-canned fruit, or a gathering of flowers from the garden—just whatever is blooming at the time. So the summertime pastels from a pre-cut 10" layer cake were just the right choice.

Finished Size: $61^3/_4$" x $61^3/_4$" (157 cm x 157 cm)
Finished Dresden Plate Block Size: $9^1/_2$" x $9^1/_2$" (24 cm x 24 cm)
Finished Four-Patch Block Size: $5^5/_8$" x $5^5/_8$" (14 cm x 14 cm)

fabric requirements

Yardage is based on 43"/44" (109 cm/112 cm) wide fabric.

1 Layer Cake or 39 assorted squares 10" x 10" (25 cm x 25 cm) for Dresden Plate and alternate blocks
$^3/_8$ yd (34 cm) of pink print for Dresden Plate centers
1 yd (91 cm) of cream print for Dresden Plate background squares
$^3/_8$ yd (34 cm) of green plaid for Four-Patch blocks
1 yd (91 cm) of green print for Four-Patch blocks and outer borders
$^7/_8$ yd (80 cm) of green dot print for inner borders and binding
$3^7/_8$ yds (3.5 m) of fabric for backing

You will also need:

$69^3/_4$" x $69^3/_4$" (177 cm x 177 cm) piece of batting
Heat-resistant template plastic
Freezer paper

organizing the pre-cuts

From Charm Pack or assorted squares:

- Select 13 large print squares for alternate blocks.
- Select 16 medium/dark squares for Dresden Plate wedges.
- Select 10 light/medium squares for Four-Patch blocks.

cutting the pieces

*Follow **Rotary Cutting**, page 70, to cut fabric. Cut all strips from the selvage-to-selvage width of the fabric. All measurements include 1/4" seam allowances. Refer to **Making Templates**, page 71, to make templates from wedge and circle patterns, page 69.*

From medium/dark squares:

- Cut 192 **wedges**.

From *each* light/medium square:

- Cut 2 strips 2 1/2" wide. From these strips, cut 80 **small squares** 2 1/2" x 2 1/2".

From pink print:

- Cut 12 **circles** using circle template.

From cream print:

- Cut 3 strips 10" wide. From these strips, cut 12 **background squares** 10" x 10".

From green plaid:

- Cut 3 strips 3 3/4" wide. From these strips, cut 24 squares 3 3/4" x 3 3/4". Cut each square once diagonally to make 48 **corner triangles**.

From green print:

- Cut 2 strips 3 3/4" wide. From these strips, cut 16 squares 3 3/4" x 3 3/4". Cut each square once diagonally to make 32 **corner triangles**.
- Cut 4 **outer borders** 6 1/8" x 27 1/2".

From green dot:

- Cut 2 **top/bottom inner borders** 1 1/2" x 50", piecing as necessary.
- Cut 2 **side inner borders** 1 1/2" x 48", piecing as necessary.
- Cut 7 **binding strips** 2 1/2" wide.

making the blocks

*Follow **Piecing And Pressing**, page 71, to make the Blocks. Match right sides and use 1/4" seam allowances throughout.*

dresden plate blocks

1. Fold 1 **background square** in half horizontally, vertically, and diagonally. Finger press folds to crease: unfold (FIG. 1).
2. Matching right sides, sew 2 **wedges** together to make UNIT 1. Make 8 Unit 1's.
3. Sew 4 Unit 1's together to make UNIT 2. Make 2 Unit 2's.

FIG. 1

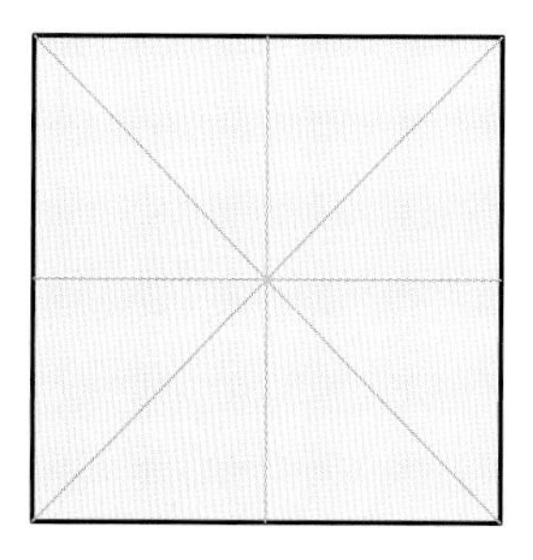

UNIT 1 (MAKE 8)

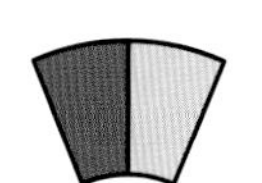

UNIT 2 (MAKE 2)

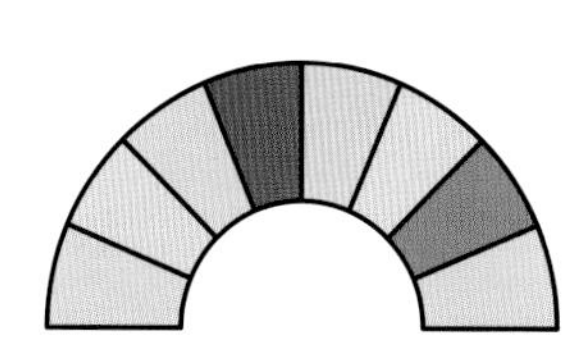

DRESDEN PLATE

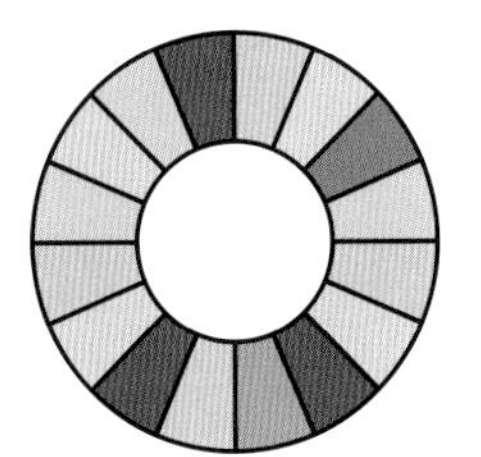

FIG. 2

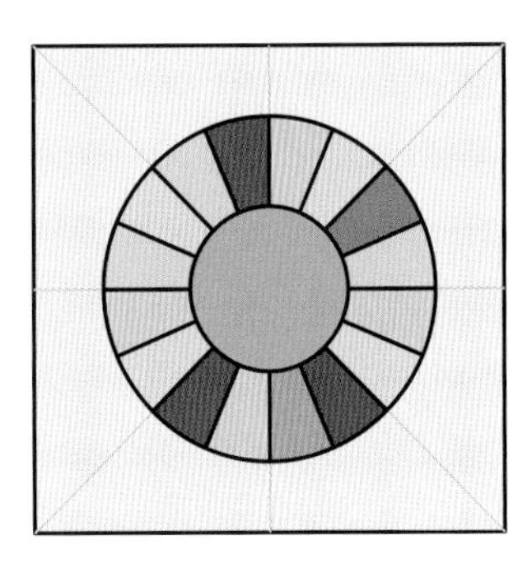

DRESDEN PLATE BLOCK (MAKE 12)

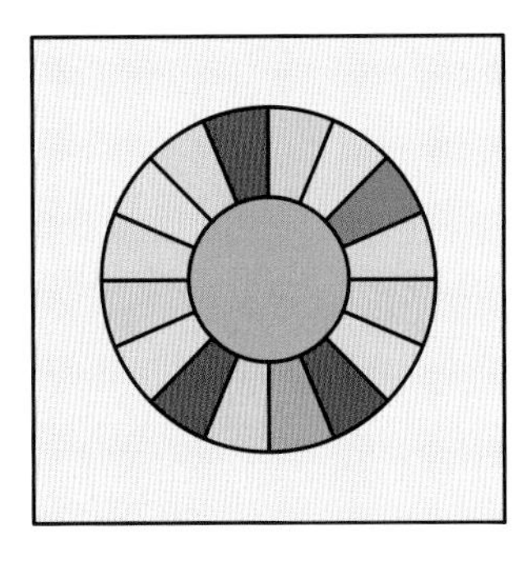

BLOCK CENTER (MAKE 20)

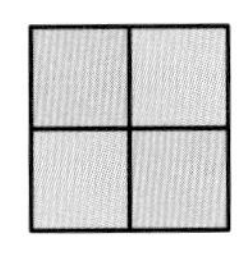

FOUR-PATCH BLOCK (MAKE 20)

ROW 1 (MAKE 3)

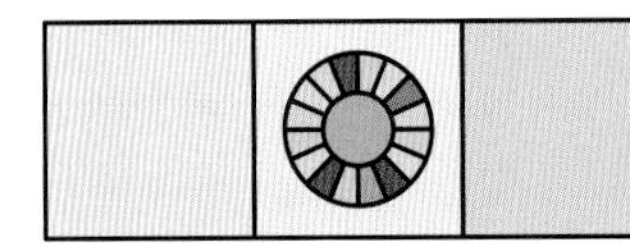

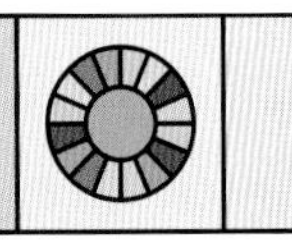

ROW 2 (MAKE 2)

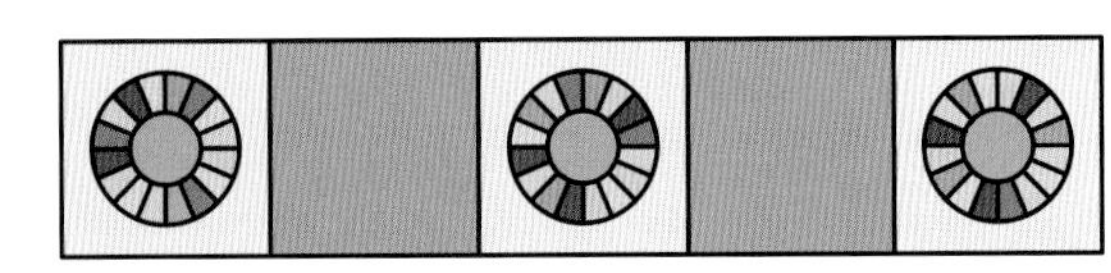

4. Sew 2 Unit 2's together to make a DRESDEN PLATE.
5. Using **large circle pattern**, page 69, cut 1 large circle from freezer paper. With shiny side down, center and press large circle to wrong side of Dresden Plate. Press seam allowance of Dresden Plate over freezer paper circle. Remove freezer paper circle.
6. Center Dresden Plate on background square and align seams in plate with creases; pin plate in place (FIG. 2).
7. Use a Blindstitch, page 78, to appliqué outer edge of Dresden Plate to background square.
8. Using dashed line of **circle pattern**, page 69, as cutting line, repeat Step 5 to cut a freezer paper circle and prepare **circle** for appliquéing.
9. Covering inner raw edges, center circle on Dresden Plate. Repeat Step 6 to appliqué circle in place to make DRESDEN PLATE BLOCK. Make 12 Dresden Plate Blocks.

four-patch blocks

*For each Four-Patch Block, select 2 light like fabric small squares, 2 medium like fabric small squares, and 4 green plaid **or** green print corner triangles.*

1. Sew 2 light and 2 medium like fabric **small squares** together to make BLOCK CENTER. Make 20 Block Centers.
2. Sew 1 **corner triangle** to opposite sides of a block center. Sew 1 corner triangle to each remaining side to make FOUR-PATCH BLOCK. Make 12 Four-Patch Blocks with green plaid corner triangles and 8 with green print corner triangles. Square Blocks to 6$^{1}/_{8}$" x 6$^{1}/_{8}$".

assembling the quilt top center

Refer to QUILT TOP DIAGRAM *for placement.*

1. Sew 2 Dresden Plate Blocks and 3 alternate blocks together to make ROW 1. Make 3 Row 1's.
2. Sew 3 Dresden Plate Blocks and 2 alternate blocks together to make ROW 2. Make 3 Row 2's.
3. Alternating Rows 1 and 2, sew Rows together to make QUILT TOP CENTER.

adding the borders

1. Sew **side** then **top/bottom inner borders** to Quilt Top Center.
2. For SIDE OUTER BORDERS, sew 2 Four-Patch blocks to each short edge of 2 **outer borders**. For TOP/BOTTOM OUTER BORDERS, sew 3 Four-Patch blocks to each short edge of 2 remaining **outer borders**.
3. Matching centers and corners, sew Side then Top/Bottom Outer Borders to Quilt Top Center.

SIDE OUTER BORDER (MAKE 2)

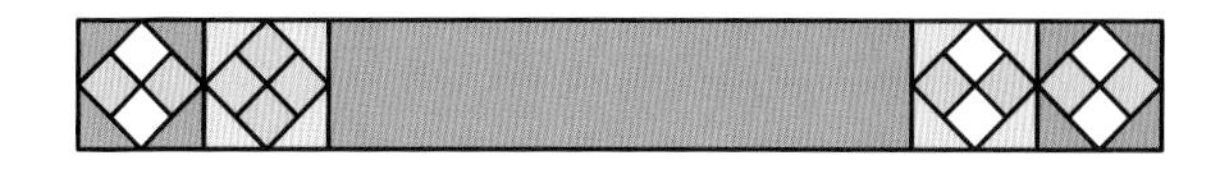

TOP/BOTTOM OUTER BORDER (MAKE 2)

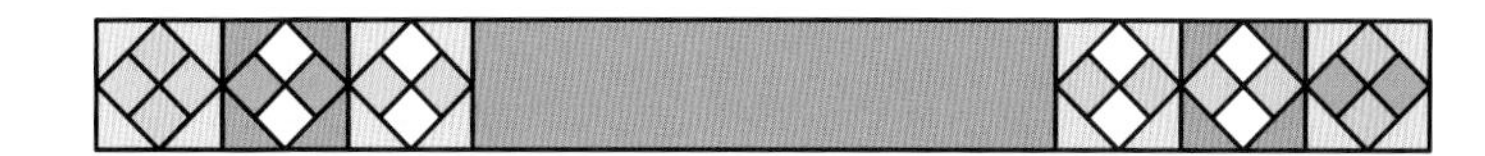

completing the quilt

1. Follow **Quilting**, page 74, to layer and quilt as desired. My quilt is machine quilted with a meandering loop pattern in the Block backgrounds. There is outline quilting in each wedge and a flower motif in the center of each Dresden Plate. The inner border has a wave and loop design. The Four-Patch blocks are quilted with a petal in each square and a loop in each triangle. There are leaves quilted in the remainder of the outer border.
2. Refer to **Making A Hanging Sleeve**, page 75, to make and attach a hanging sleeve, if desired.
3. Use **binding strips** and follow **Making Double-Fold Binding,** page 76, to make **binding**. Follow **Attaching Binding**, page 76, to bind quilt.

QUILT TOP DIAGRAM

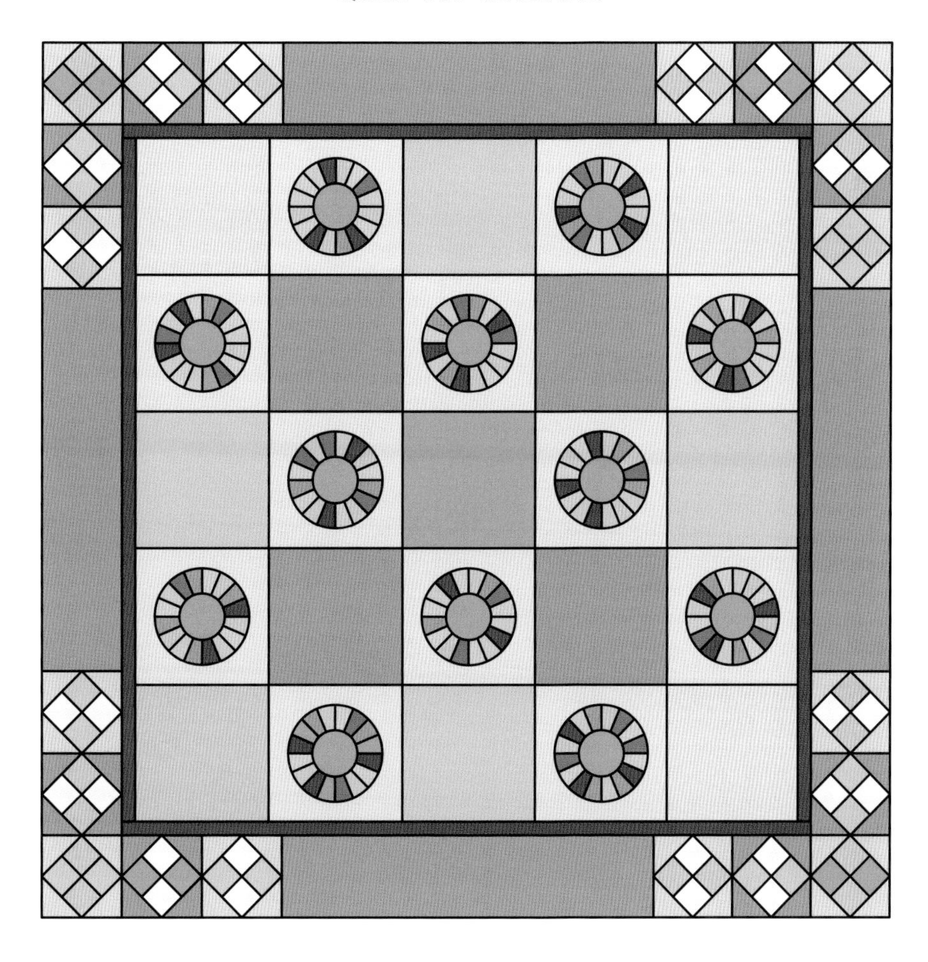

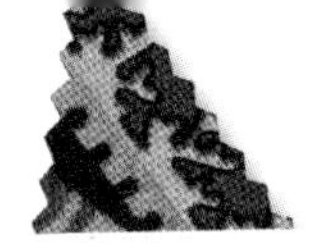

bozley's TRIANGLES

For this quilt, I enlisted the piecing skills of my friend, Sue Graham. Not to be left out of the fun, Sue's grand-dog Bozley decided to "help." He knocked over both of her design walls, sending hundreds of triangles fluttering all over the floor! Thank goodness Sue had photographed the layout and was able to put it back together!

quilt

Finished Size: 52$^1/_2$" x 52$^1/_2$" (133 cm x 133 cm)
Finished Block Size: 8" x 8" (20 cm x 20 cm)

fabric requirements

Yardage is based on 43"/44" (109 cm/112 cm) wide fabric.

1 Jelly Roll ***or*** 40 assorted strips 2$^1/_2$" x 40" (6 cm x 102 cm) for blocks
$^1/_4$ yd (23 cm) **each** of 2 different blue prints for blocks
$^1/_4$ yd (23 cm) **each** of 3 different dark blue prints for blocks
$^7/_8$ yd (80 cm) of 1 dark blue tone-on-tone print for blocks and outer border blocks
$^1/_2$ yd (46 cm) of navy star print with 1$^1/_2$"wide stars for outer border
$^3/_8$ yd (34 cm) of gold print for inner border
$^1/_4$ yd (23 cm) of gold/blue stripe for middle border
$^1/_2$ yd (46 cm) of red print for binding
3$^1/_2$ yds (3.2 m) of fabric for backing

You will also need:

Omnigrid® Ruler #96
61" x 61" (155 cm x 155 cm) piece of batting

organizing the pre-cuts

From Jelly Roll *or* assorted strips:

- Divide the strips into blue prints, dark blue prints, tan/gold prints, and red prints.

cutting the pieces

Follow ***Rotary Cutting****, page 70, to cut fabric. Cut all strips from the selvage-to-selvage width of the fabric. All measurements include 1/4" seam allowances. After cutting* ***strips****, sort the strips as you did the Jelly Roll and combine cut strips and Jelly Roll strips.*

From *each* blue print:
- Cut 3 **strips** 2 1/2" wide.

From *each* dark blue print:
- Cut 3 **strips** 2 1/2" wide.

From dark blue tone-on-tone print:
- Cut 4 **outer borders** 4" x 31 1/2".
- Cut 4 **strips** 2 1/2" wide.

From navy star print:
- Cut 20 **squares** 3" x 3" with 1 star centered in each square.

From gold print:
- Cut 2 **side inner borders** 2" x 40 1/2".
- Cut 2 **top/bottom inner borders** 2" x 43 1/2", pieced as necessary.

From gold/blue stripe:
- Cut 2 **side middle borders** 1 1/4" x 43 1/2", pieced as necessary.
- Cut 2 **top/bottom middle borders** 1 1/4" x 45", pieced as necessary.

From red print:
- Cut 6 **binding strips** 2 1/2" wide.

cutting the blocks

When instructed to cut ***triangles****, use Omnigrid Ruler #96 and follow manufacturer's instructions for 2"* ***finished*** *triangles. Keep pieces together for each block.*

For *each* Star Block (12 blocks) from like fabric strips, cut:
- 12 like fabric **dark blue triangles (set 1)**.
- 4 like fabric **dark blue triangles (set 2)**.
- 10 like fabric **tan/gold triangles (set 3)**.
- 6 like fabric **tan/gold triangles (set 4)**.

For *each* Pinwheel Block (13 blocks), from fabric strips, cut:
- 12 like fabric **blue triangles (set 5)**.
- 8 like fabric **tan/gold triangles (set 6)**.
- 8 like fabric **tan/gold triangles (set 7)**.
- 4 like fabric **red print triangles (set 8)**.

For Square-In-A-Square Blocks (20 blocks) cut:
- 80 **assorted tan/gold print triangles**.

making the blocks

Follow ***Piecing And Pressing****, page 71, to make the Blocks. Match right sides and use 1/4" seam allowances throughout.*

star blocks

1. Matching long edges, sew 1 **set 1 triangle** and 1 **set 3 triangle** together to make TRIANGLE-SQUARE A. Make 6 Triangle-Square A's.

TRIANGLE-SQUARE A (MAKE 6)

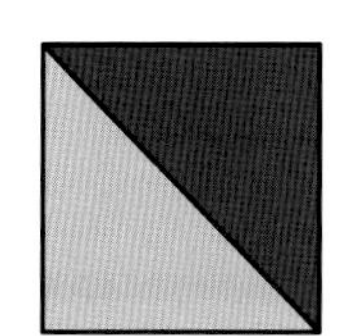

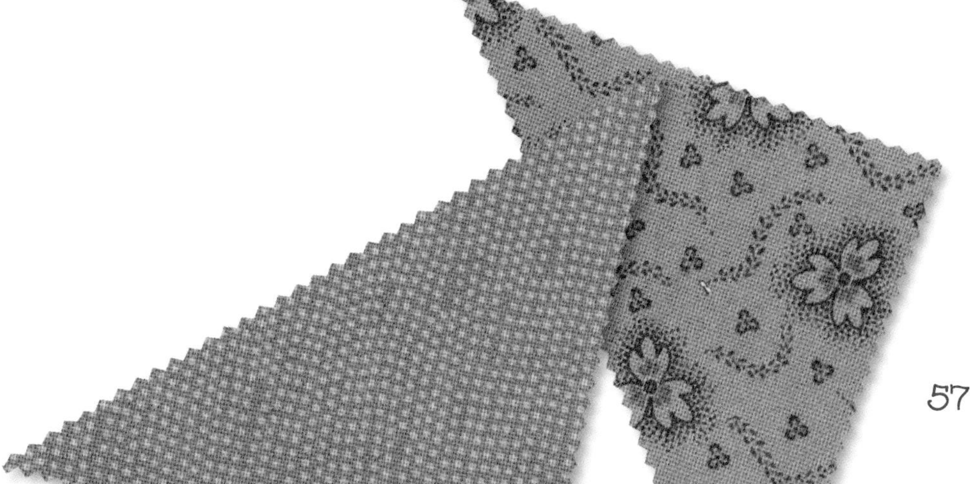

TRIANGLE-SQUARE B
(MAKE 6)

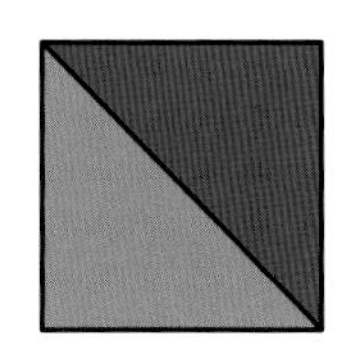

TRIANGLE-SQUARE C
(MAKE 4)

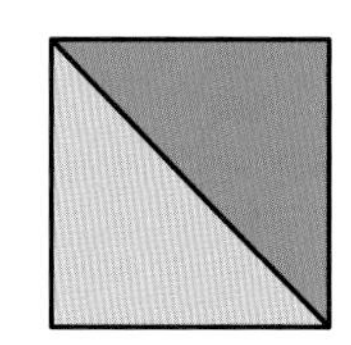

BLOCK ASSEMBLY DIAGRAM

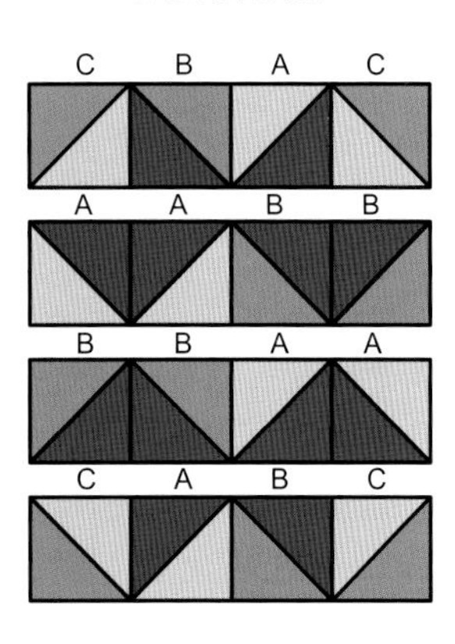

STAR BLOCK
(MAKE 12)

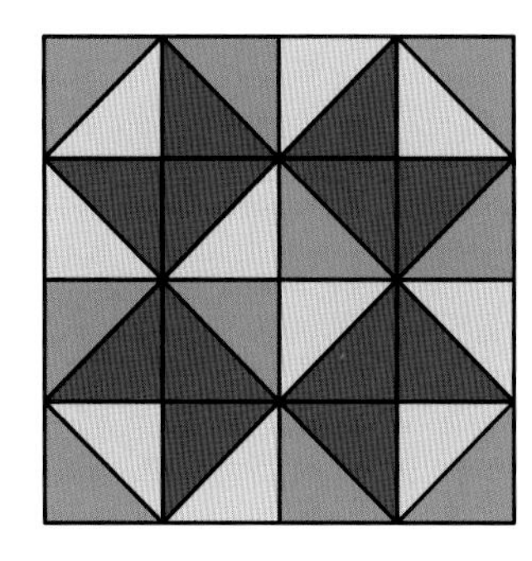

TRIANGLE-SQUARE D (MAKE 4)

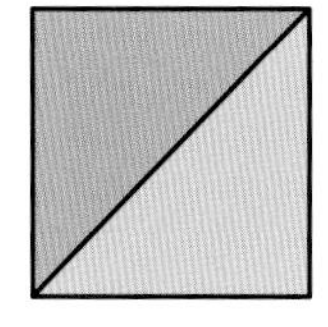

TRIANGLE-SQUARE E
(MAKE 8)

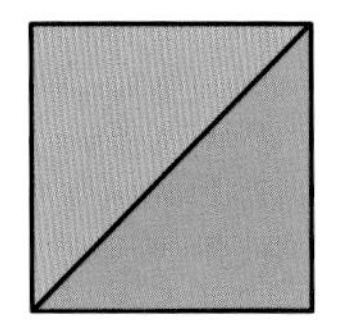

TRIANGLE-SQUARE F
(MAKE 4)

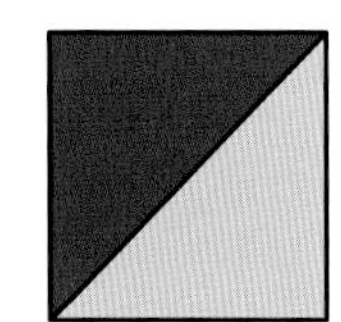

BLOCK ASSEMBLY DIAGRAM

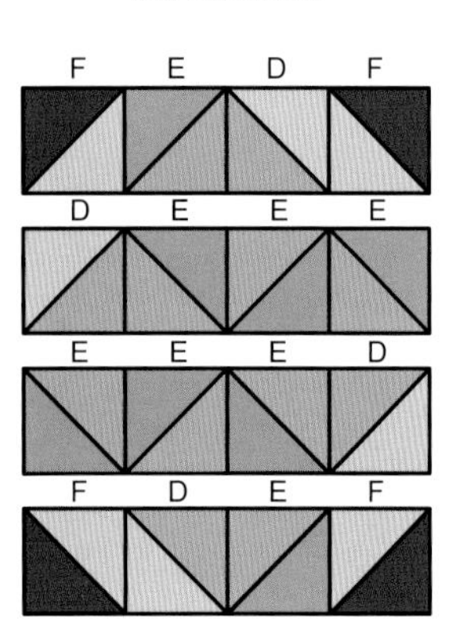

PINWHEEL BLOCK
(MAKE 13)

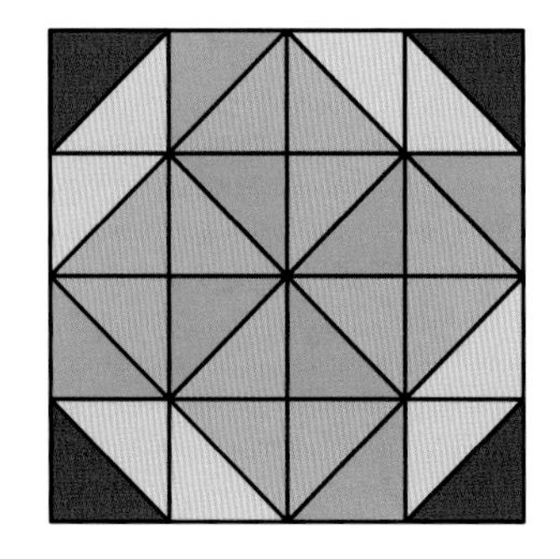

2. Matching long edges, sew 1 **set 1 triangle** and 1 **set 4 triangle** together to make TRIANGLE- SQUARE B. Make 6 Triangle-Square B's.
3. Matching long edges, sew 1 **set 2 triangle** and 1 **set 3 triangle** together to make TRIANGLE- SQUARE C. Make 4 Triangle-Square C's.
4. Refer to BLOCK ASSEMBLY DIAGRAM to sew Triangle-Squares together to make STAR BLOCK. Make 12 Star Blocks.

pinwheel blocks

1. Matching long edges, sew 1 **set 5 triangle** and 1 **set 6 triangle** together to make TRIANGLE- SQUARE D. Make 4 Triangle-Square D's.
2. Matching long edges, sew 1 **set 5 triangle** and 1 **set 7 triangle** together to make TRIANGLE- SQUARE E. Make 8 Triangle-Square E's.
3. Matching long edges, sew 1 **set 8 triangle** and 1 **set 6 triangle** together to make TRIANGLE- SQUARE F. Make 4 Triangle-Square F's.
4. Refer to BLOCK ASSEMBLY DIAGRAM to sew Triangle-Squares together to make PINWHEEL BLOCK. Make 13 Pinwheel Blocks.

square-in-a-square blocks

For each block you will need, 1 navy star print square and 4 assorted tan/gold print triangles.

1. Matching long edges, sew 1 assorted tan print **triangle** to opposite sides of a star print **square**; press open.
2. Matching long edges, sew 1 assorted tan print triangle to each remaining side of a star print square to make SQUARE-IN-A-SQUARE BLOCK. Trim Square-In-A-Square Block to $3^1/_2$" x $3^1/_2$". Make 20 Square-In-A-Square Blocks.

assembling the quilt top center

Refer to QUILT TOP DIAGRAM*, page 60, for placement.*

1. Sew 3 Pinwheel and 2 Star Blocks together to make ROW 1. Make 3 Row 1's.
2. Sew 2 Pinwheel and 3 Star Blocks together to make ROW 2. Make 2 Row 2's.
3. Alternating Rows 1 and 2, sew Rows together to make QUILT TOP CENTER.

adding the borders

1. Sew **side** then **top/bottom inner borders** to Quilt Top Center.
2. Sew **side** then **top/bottom middle borders** to Quilt Top Center.
3. For SIDE OUTER BORDERS, sew 2 Square-In-A-Square blocks to each short edge of 2 **outer borders**. For TOP/BOTTOM OUTER BORDERS, sew 3 Square-In-A-Square blocks to each short edge of 2 remaining **outer borders**.
4. Matching centers and corners, sew Side then Top/Bottom Outer Borders to Quilt Top Center.

SQUARE-IN-A-SQUARE BLOCK (MAKE 20)

ROW 1 (MAKE 3)

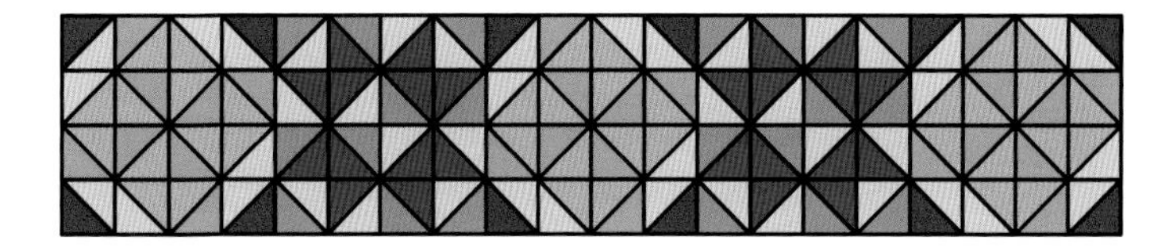

ROW 2 (MAKE 2)

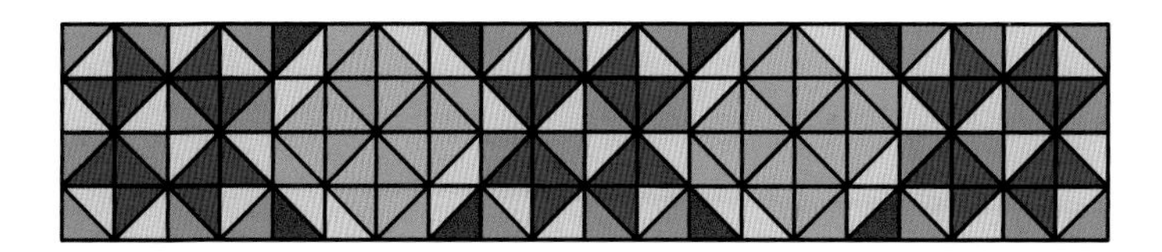

SIDE OUTER BORDER (MAKE 2)

TOP/BOTTOM OUTER BORDER (MAKE 2)

completing the quilt

1. Follow **Quilting**, page 74, to layer and quilt as desired. My quilt is machine quilted with loops in the Pinwheel Blocks and alternating straight and wavy lines in the Star Blocks. The inner and middle borders are quilted with a wide zigzag and the outer border repeats the alternating straight and wavy lines of the Star Blocks.
2. Refer to **Making A Hanging Sleeve**, page 75, to make and attach a hanging sleeve, if desired.
3. Use **binding strips** and follow **Making Double-Fold Binding,** page 76, to make **binding**. Follow **Attaching Binding**, page 76, to bind quilt.

QUILT TOP DIAGRAM

pillow

Finished Size: 18" x 18" (46 cm x 46 cm) excluding binding
Finished Block Size: 8" x 8" (20 cm x 20 cm)

fabric requirements

Yardage is based on 43"/44" (109 cm/112 cm) wide fabric. The pillow is made using strips leftover from the quilt.

1 blue print strip 2 1/2" x 18" (6 cm x 46 cm) for block
2 tan/gold print strips 2 1/2" x 12" (6 cm x 30 cm) for block
16 assorted tan/gold print scraps 2 1/2" x 3" (6 cm x 8 cm) for outer border blocks
3 assorted red print strips 2 1/2" x 6" (6 cm x 15 cm) for block and inner border
1/4 yd (23 cm) of red print for binding
1/8 yd (11 cm) of green print for inner border
4 squares *each* 3" x 3" (8 cm x 8 cm) cut from navy star print with 1 1/2" wide star centered in square for outer border
1/4 yd (23 cm) of blue stripe for outer border
3/8 yd (34 cm) dark blue print for pillow back

You will also need:

Omnigrid® Ruler #96
22" x 22" (56 cm x 56 cm) piece of batting
18" x 18" (46 cm x 46 cm) pillow form

cutting the pieces

*Follow **Rotary Cutting**, page 70, to cut fabric. Cut all strips from the selvage-to-selvage width of the fabric. All measurements include $^1/_4$" seam allowances. When instructed to cut **triangles**, use Omnigrid Ruler #96 and follow manufacturer's instructions for 2" **finished** triangles.*

From blue print strip:
- Cut 12 like fabric **triangles (set 5)**.

From tan/gold print strips:
- Cut 8 like fabric **triangles (set 6)**.
- Cut 8 like fabric **triangles (set 7)**.

From assorted tan scraps:
- Cut 16 **triangles**.

From *each* assorted red print strip:
- Cut 4 like fabric **triangles.** From these triangles, choose 4 like fabric triangles for Block **(set 8)**.

From red print:
- Cut 3 **binding strips** $1^1/_2$" wide.

From green print:
- Cut 1 strip $2^7/_8$" wide. From this strip, cut 2 squares $2^7/_8$" x $2^7/_8$". Cut each square in half once diagonally to make 4 **corner triangles**.
- Cut 12 **triangles**.

From blue stripe:
- Cut 4 **outer borders** 4" x $11^1/_2$".

From dark blue print:
- Cut 2 **pillow backs** $12^3/_4$" x $18^1/_2$".

PINWHEEL BLOCK (MAKE 1)

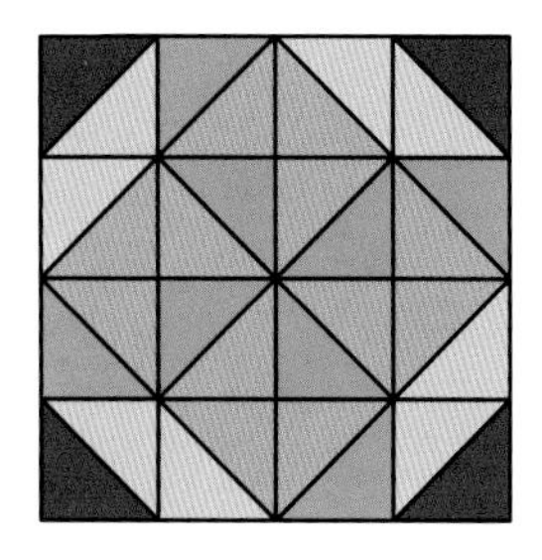

PILLOW TOP CENTER

INNER BORDER (MAKE 4)

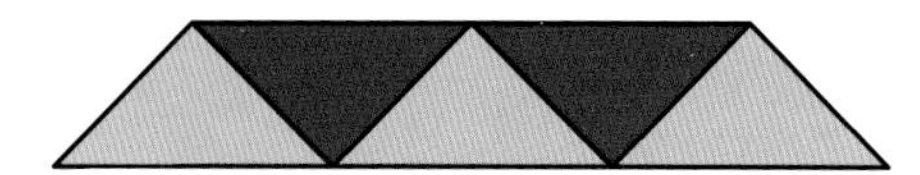

SQUARE-IN-A-SQUARE BLOCK (MAKE 4)

making the pillow top

*Follow **Piecing And Pressing**, page 71, to make the Pillow Top. Match right sides and use $^1/_4$" seam allowances throughout.*

1. Follow **Pinwheel Blocks**, page 58, to make 1 PINWHEEL BLOCK.
2. Matching short edges and alternating orientation, sew 3 **green print** and 2 **red print triangles** together to make INNER BORDER. Make 4 Inner Borders.
3. Matching centers, sew 1 Inner Border to opposite sides of Pinwheel Block; open and press. **Note:** Border will extend beyond edge of Block. Block will "float" when all 4 borders are attached. Sew 1 Inner Border to each remaining side of Pinwheel Block.
4. Sew 1 **corner triangle** to each corner of Pinwheel Block to make PILLOW TOP CENTER.

5. Using **assorted tan triangles** and **blue squares,** follow **Square-In-A-Square Blocks**, page 59, to make SQUARE-IN-A-SQUARE BLOCK. Make 4 Square-In-A-Square Blocks.
6. Matching centers and corners and easing to fit, sew 1 **outer border** to opposite sides of Pillow Top Center.
7. Sew 1 Square-In-A-Square Block to each short edge of remaining outer borders. Matching centers and corners and easing to fit, sew outer borders to top and bottom edges of Pillow Top Center.

completing the pillow

1. Follow **Quilting**, page 74, to layer and quilt the batting and pillow top. My Pillow Top is machine quilted with an all-over flower and leaf design.
2. Press 1 long edge of each **pillow back** $^{1}/_{4}$" to the wrong side twice. Topstitch hem close to the folded edges.
3. With right sides facing up, overlap the two hemmed edges of the pillow backs until the overall measurement is $18^{1}/_{2}$" x $18^{1}/_{2}$". Baste the overlapped edges together.
4. Matching wrong sides, baste the Pillow Top and back together $^{1}/_{2}$" from raw edge. Trim batting even with Pillow Top.
5. To curve corners, place a small glass on one corner of Pillow Top (FIG. 1). Draw around glass; repeat to mark each corner. Trim Pillow Top, batting and pillow back along drawn lines.
6. Use **binding strips** and follow **Making Double-Fold Binding,** page 76, to make **binding**.
7. Matching raw edges of binding to raw edges of Pillow Top, pin binding to right side of Pillow Top.

FIG. 1

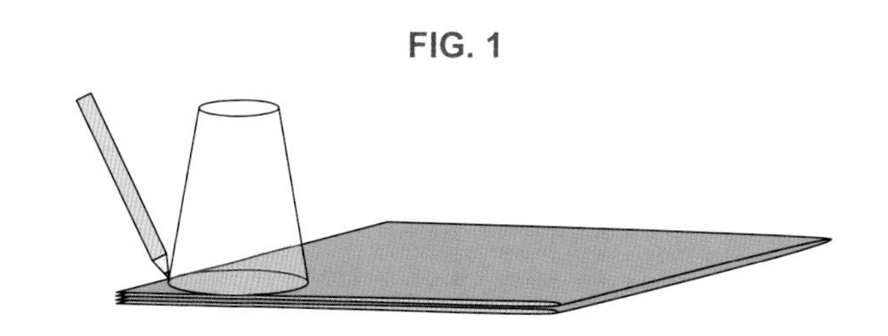

PILLOW TOP DIAGRAM

8. Beginning approximately 10" from end of binding and using a $^{1}/_{4}$" seam allowance, sew binding to Pillow Top, stopping approximately 10" from starting point (Fig. 25, page 77).
9. Follow Steps 7-12 and 14-15 of **Attaching Binding**, page 77, to finish binding Pillow Top. Remove basting threads and insert pillow form.

i REMEMBER

Oh, the memories this quilt evokes with its retro-look fabrics! I think I may have had a dress in fabric very similar to one of the dark blue prints. Zipping through the piecing of this project was as much fun as the stroll down memory lane.

Finished Size: 57" x 57" (145 cm x 145 cm)
Finished Block Size: 8" x 8" (20 cm x 20 cm)

fabric requirements

Yardage is based on 43"/44" (109 cm/112 cm) wide fabric.

1 Jelly Roll ***or*** 26 assorted strips $2^1/_2$" x 40" (6 cm x 102 cm) for checkerboard blocks
2 Charm Packs ***or*** 50 assorted light/medium squares 5" x 5" (13 cm x 13 cm) for pinwheel blocks
$^5/_8$ yd (57 cm) of red print for pinwheel blocks
$1^1/_4$ yds (1.1 m) of blue print for pinwheel blocks and binding
$3^5/_8$ yds (3.3 m) of fabric for backing

You will also need:

65" x 65" (165 cm x 165 cm) piece of batting

organizing the pre-cuts

From Jelly Roll *or* assorted strips:

- Select 13 **light** and 13 **medium/dark strips**.

From Charm Packs or assorted squares:

- Select 50 light/medium squares. Cut squares in half once diagonally to make 100 **triangles**.

CABIN

cutting the pieces

*Follow **Rotary Cutting**, page 70, to cut fabric. Cut all strips from the selvage-to-selvage width of the fabric. All measurements include $^1/_4$" seam allowances.*

From Jelly Roll *or* assorted strips:

- Cut each strip in half to make 26 **light** and 26 **dark strips** $2^1/_2$" x 20".

From red print:

- Cut 4 strips 5" wide. From these strips, cut 25 squares 5" x 5". Cut each square in half once diagonally to make 50 **red triangles.**

From blue print:

- Cut 4 strips 5" wide. From these strips, cut 25 squares 5" x 5". Cut each square once diagonally to make 50 **blue triangles**.
- Cut 7 **binding strips** $2^1/_2$" wide.

making the blocks

*Follow **Piecing And Pressing**, page 71, to make the Blocks. Match right sides and use $^1/_4$" seam allowances throughout.*

checkerboard block

1. Matching long edges sew 1 **light** and 1 **medium/dark strip** together to make STRIP SET. Make 25 Strip Sets. Cut across Strip Sets at $2^1/_2$" intervals to make UNIT 1's. Make 192 Unit 1's.
2. Sew 2 Unit 1's together to make UNIT 2. Make 96 Unit 2's.
3. Sew 4 Unit 2's together to make CHECKERBOARD BLOCK. Make 24 Checkerboard Blocks.

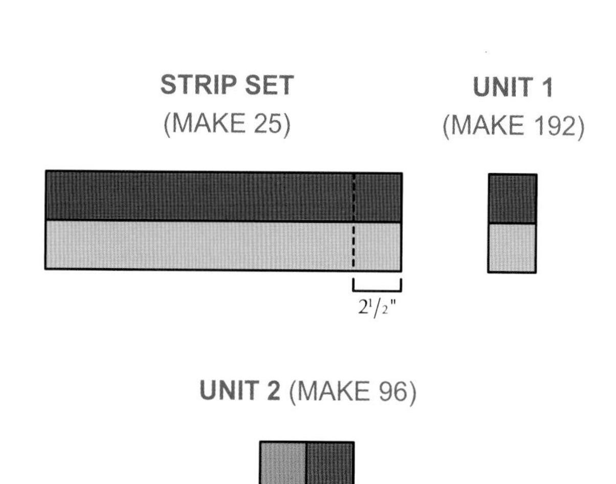

CHECKERBOARD BLOCK (MAKE 24)

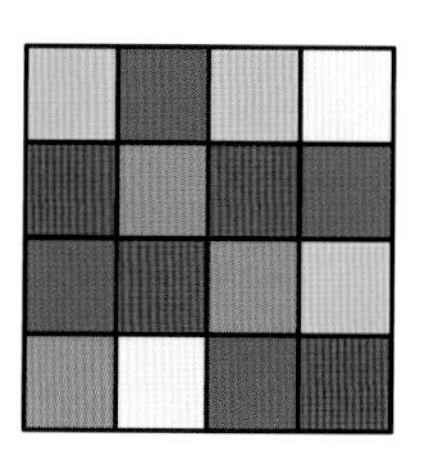

TRIANGLE-SQUARE A (MAKE 50)

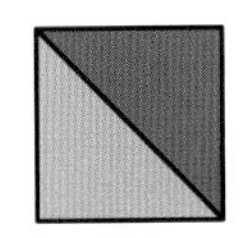

TRIANGLE-SQUARE B (MAKE 50)

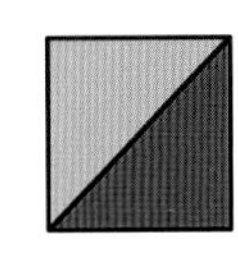

PINWHEEL BLOCK (MAKE 25)

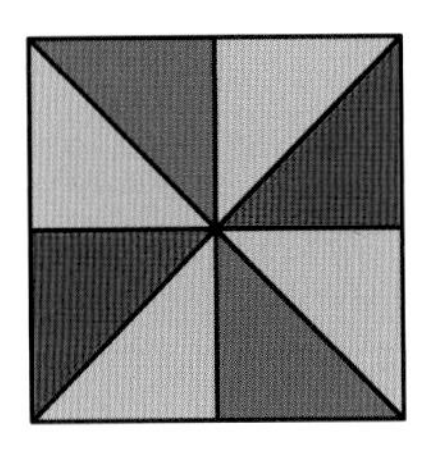

ROW 1 (MAKE 4)

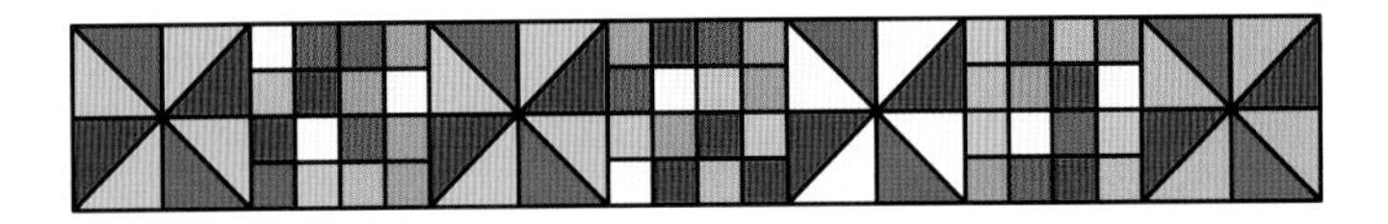

ROW 2 (MAKE 3)

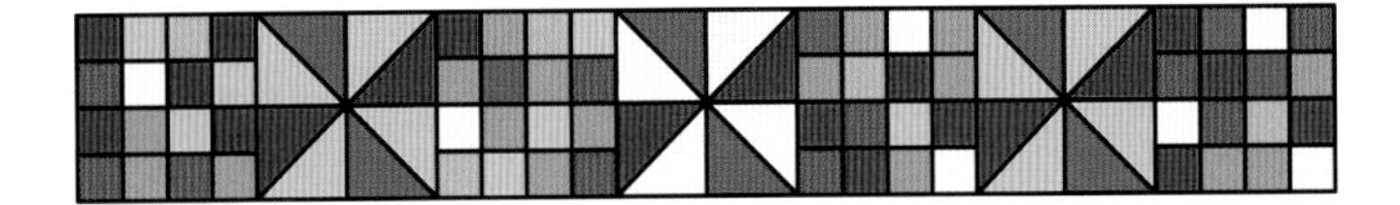

pinwheel block

*For **each** block you will need 2 red, 2 blue, and 4 light/medium triangles.*

1. Sew 1 **blue** and 1 **light/medium triangle** together to make TRIANGLE-SQUARE A. Make 50 Triangle-Square A's. Trim Triangle-Square A's to $4^1/_2$" x $4^1/_2$".
2. Sew 1 **red** and 1 **light/medium triangle** together to make TRIANGLE-SQUARE B. Make 50 Triangle-Square B's. Trim Triangle-Square B's to $4^1/_2$" x $4^1/_2$".
3. Sew 2 Triangle-Square A's and 2 Triangle-Square B's together to make PINWHEEL BLOCK. Make 25 Pinwheel Blocks.

assembling the quilt top

1. Sew 3 Checkerboard and 4 Pinwheel Blocks together to make ROW 1. Make 4 Row 1's.
2. Sew 4 Checkerboard and 3 Pinwheel Blocks together to make ROW 2. Make 3 Row 2's.
3. Alternating Rows 1 and 2, sew Rows together to make QUILT TOP.

completing the quilt

1. Follow **Quilting**, page 74, to layer and quilt as desired. My quilt is machine quilted with echoing circles in the Checkerboard Blocks and spinning pinwheels in the Pinwheel Blocks.
2. Refer to **Making A Hanging Sleeve**, page 75, to make and attach a hanging sleeve, if desired.
3. Use **binding strips** and follow **Making Double-Fold Binding**, page 76, to make **binding**. Follow **Attaching Binding**, page 76, to bind quilt.

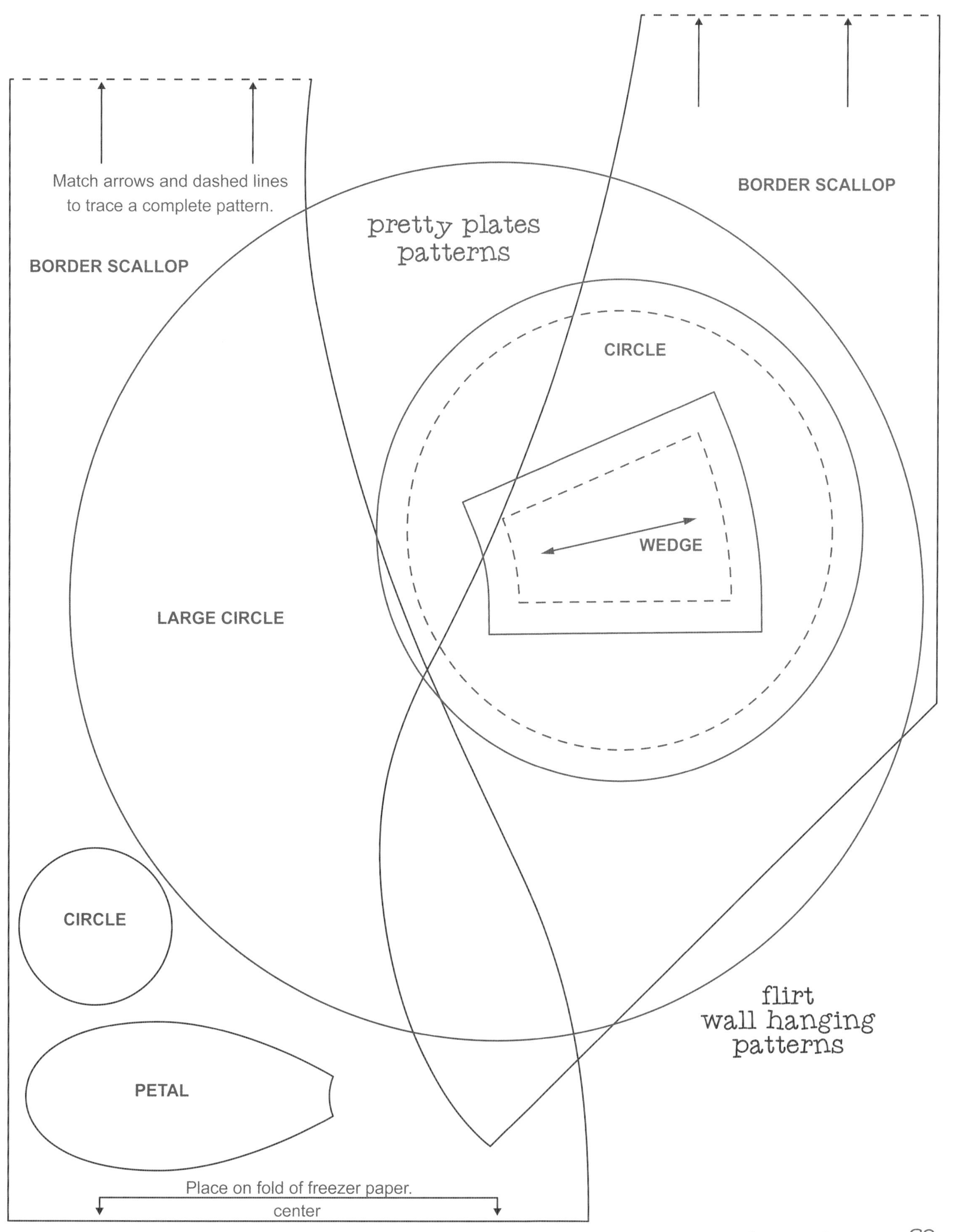
Match arrows and dashed lines
to trace a complete pattern.
BORDER SCALLOP
pretty plates
patterns
BORDER SCALLOP
CIRCLE
WEDGE
LARGE CIRCLE
CIRCLE
flirt
wall hanging
patterns
PETAL
Place on fold of freezer paper.
center

general INSTRUCTIONS

To make your quilting **easier** and more **enjoyable**, we encourage you to **carefully read** all of the general instructions, study the **color photographs**, and familiarize yourself with the individual project instructions before beginning a project.

fabrics

selecting fabrics

Choose high-quality, medium-weight 100% cotton fabrics. All-cotton fabrics hold a crease better, fray less, and are easier to quilt than cotton/polyester blends.

Yardage requirements listed for each project are based on 43"/44" wide fabric with a "usable" width of 40" after shrinkage and trimming selvages. Actual usable width will probably vary slightly from fabric to fabric. Our recommended yardage lengths should be adequate for occasional re-squaring of fabric when many cuts are required.

rotary cutting

Rotary cutting has brought speed and accuracy to quiltmaking by allowing quilters to easily cut strips of fabric and then cut those strips into smaller pieces.

- Place fabric on work surface with fold closest to you.
- Cut all strips from the selvage-to-selvage width of the fabric unless otherwise indicated in project instructions.
- Square left edge of fabric using rotary cutter and rulers (FIGS. 1 - 2).
- To cut each strip required for a project, place ruler over cut edge of fabric, aligning desired marking on ruler with cut edge; make cut (FIG. 3).
- When cutting several strips from a single piece of fabric, it is important to make sure that cuts remain at a perfect right angle to the fold; square fabric as needed.

FIG. 1

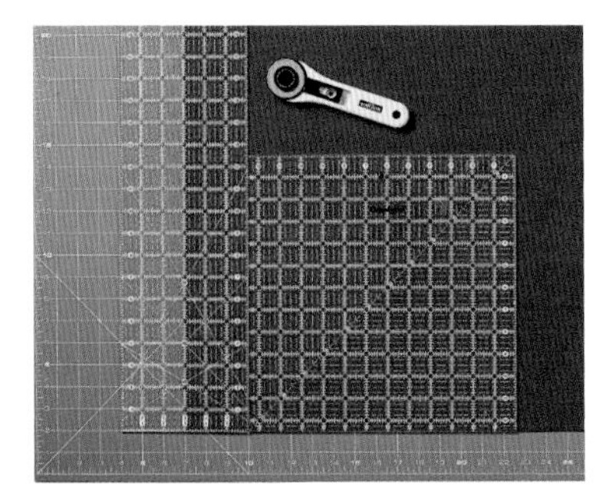

FIG. 2

FIG. 3

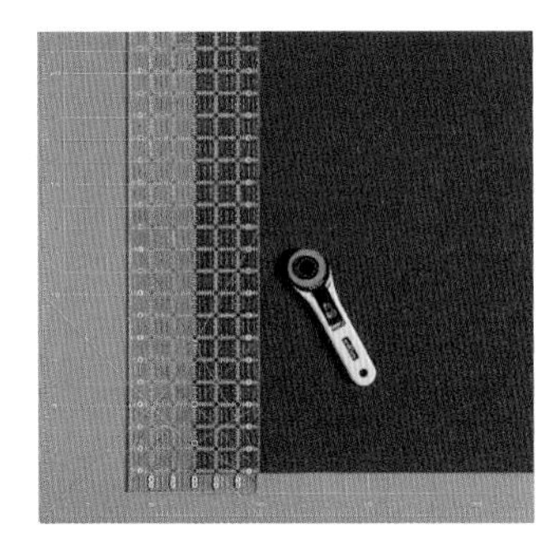

making templates

Our piecing template patterns have two lines – a solid cutting line and a dashed line showing the $^1/_4$" seam allowance.

1. To make a template from a pattern, use a permanent fine-point pen and a ruler to carefully trace pattern onto template plastic, making sure to transfer any alignment and grainline markings. Cut out template along inner edge of outer drawn line. Check template against original pattern for accuracy.
2. Place template face down on wrong side of fabric aligning grainline on template with straight grain of fabric. Use a sharp fabric-marking pencil to draw around template. Transfer all alignment markings to fabric. Cut out fabric piece using scissors or rotary cutting equipment.

piecing and pressing

Precise cutting, followed by accurate piecing, will ensure that all pieces of quilt top fit together well.

machine piecing

- Set sewing machine stitch length for approximately 11 stitches per inch.
- Use neutral-colored general-purpose sewing thread (not quilting thread) in needle and in bobbin.
- An accurate $^1/_4$" seam allowance is *essential*. Presser feet that are $^1/_4$" wide are available for most sewing machines.
- When piecing, always place pieces right sides together and match raw edges; pin if necessary.
- Chain piecing saves time and will usually result in more accurate piecing.
- Trim away points of seam allowances that extend beyond edges of sewn pieces.

sewing strip sets

When there are several strips to assemble into a strip set, first sew strips together into pairs, then sew pairs together to form strip set. To help avoid distortion, sew seams in opposite directions (FIG. 4).

sewing across seam intersections

When sewing across intersection of two seams, place pieces right sides together and match seams exactly, making sure seam allowances are pressed in opposite directions (FIG. 5).

sewing sharp points

To ensure sharp points when joining triangular or diagonal pieces, stitch across the center of the "X" (shown in pink) formed on wrong side by previous seams (FIG. 6).

FIG. 4

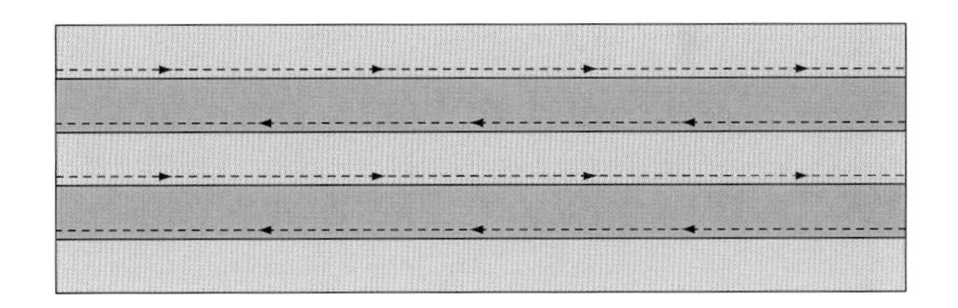

FIG. 5

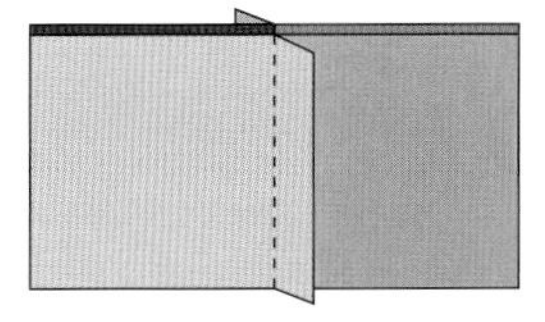

FIG. 6

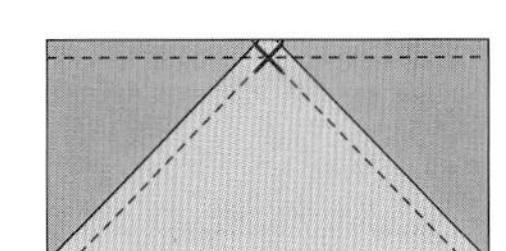

pressing

- Use steam iron set on "Cotton" for all pressing.
- Press after sewing each seam.
- Seam allowances are almost always pressed to one side, usually toward the darker fabric. However, to reduce bulk it may occasionally be necessary to press seam allowances toward the lighter fabric or even to press them open.
- To prevent a dark fabric seam allowance from showing through light fabric, trim darker seam allowance slightly narrower than lighter seam allowance.
- To press long seams, such as those in long strip sets, without curving or other distortion, lay strips across width of the ironing board.

FIG. 7

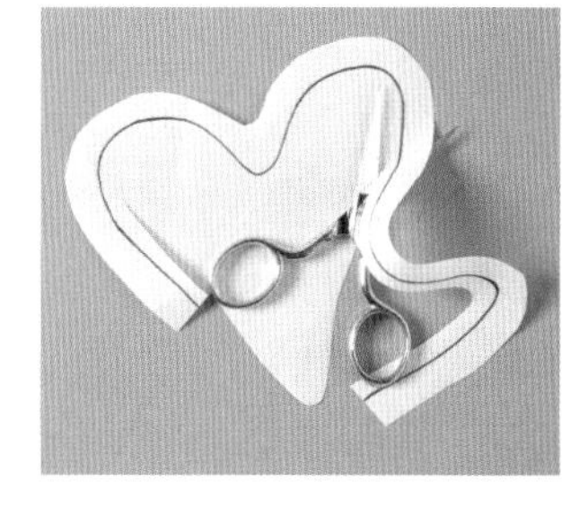

FIG. 9

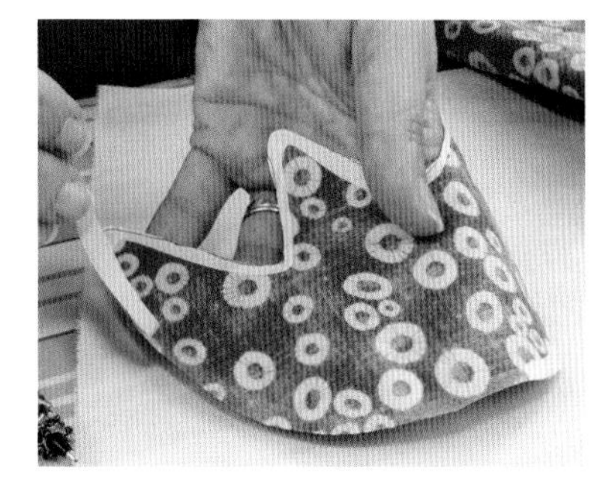

appliqué

preparing fusible appliqués

Patterns for fused appliqués are printed in reverse to enable you to use our speedy method of preparing appliqués by following **Steps 1-4** (below).

1. Place paper-backed fusible web, web side down, over appliqué pattern. Use a pencil to trace pattern onto paper side of web as many times as indicated in project instructions for a single fabric. Repeat for additional patterns and fabrics.
2. To reduce stiffness when appliquéing, cut away the center of the fusible web $^1/_4$" inside the traced line. Do not cut on the line (FIG. 7). It may not be necessary to cut away the center of small or narrow pieces.
3. Follow manufacturer's instructions to fuse traced patterns to wrong side of fabrics. Do not remove paper backing.
4. Cut out appliqué pieces along traced lines (FIG. 8). Remove paper backing from all pieces (FIG. 9).

machine appliqué

Some sewing machines feature a Blanket Stitch similar to the one used in this book. Refer to your owner's manual for machine set-up. If your machine does not have this stitch, try any of the decorative stitches your machine has until you are satisfied with the look.

1. Thread sewing machine and bobbin with 100% cotton thread in desired weight.
2. Attach an open-toe presser foot. Select far right needle position and needle down (if your machine has these features).
3. If desired, pin a commercial stabilizer to wrong side of background fabric or spray wrong side of background fabric with starch to stabilize.

4. Bring bobbin thread to the top of the fabric by lowering then raising the needle, bringing up the bobbin thread loop. Pull the loop all the way to the surface.
5. Begin by stitching 5 or 6 stitches in place (drop feed dogs or set stitch length at 0), or use your machine's lock stitch feature, if equipped, to anchor thread. Return setting to selected Blanket Stitch.
6. Most of the Blanket Stitch should be done on the appliqué with the right edges of the stitch falling at the very outside edge of the appliqué. Stitch over all exposed raw edges of appliqué pieces.
7. *(Note: Dots on **Figs. 10-14** indicate where to leave needle in fabric when pivoting.)* Always stopping with needle down in background fabric, refer to FIG. 10 to stitch outside points like tips of leaves. Stop one stitch short of point. Raise presser foot. Pivot project slightly, lower presser foot, and make on angled **Stitch 1**. Take next stitch, stop at point, and pivot so **Stitch 2** will be perpendicular to point. Pivot slightly to make **Stitch 3**. Continue stitching.
8. For outside corners (FIG. 11), stitch to corner, stopping with needle in background fabric. Raise presser foot. Pivot project, lower presser foot, and take an angled stitch. Raise presser foot. Pivot project, lower presser foot and stitch adjacent side.
9. For inside corners (FIG. 12), stitch to the corner, taking the last bite at corner and stopping with the needle down in background fabric. Raise presser foot. Pivot project, lower presser foot, and take an angled stitch. Raise presser foot. Pivot project, lower presser foot and stitch adjacent side.
10. When stitching outside curves (FIG. 13), stop with needle down in background fabric. Raise presser foot and pivot project as needed. Lower presser foot and continue stitching, pivoting as often as necessary to follow curve. Small circles may require pivoting between each stitch.
11. When stitching inside curves (FIG. 14), stop with needle down in background fabric. Raise presser foot and pivot project as needed. Lower presser foot and continue stitching, pivoting as often as necessary to follow curve.
12. When stopping stitching, use a lock stitch to sew 5 or 6 stitches in place or use a needle to pull threads to wrong side of background fabric (FIG. 15); knot, then trim ends.
13. Carefully tear away stabilizer, if used.

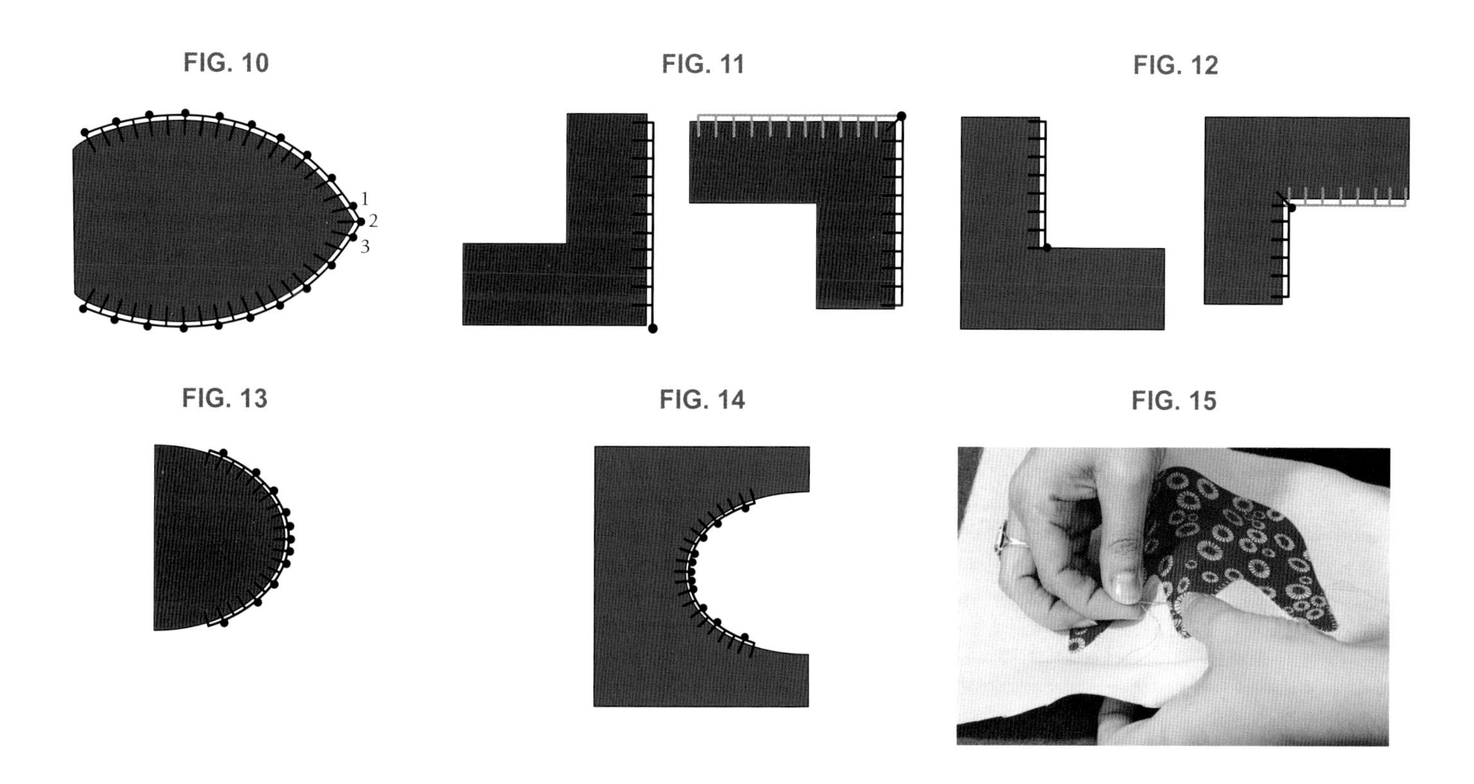

quilting

*Quilting holds the three layers (top, batting, and backing) of the quilt together. My quilts are machine quilted. Please read entire **Quilting** section, pages 74 – 75, before beginning project.*

preparing the backing

*To allow for slight shifting of quilt top during quilting, backing should be approximately 4" larger on all sides. **Note:** Backing for smaller projects such as table toppers or placemats only needs to be 2" larger on all sides. Yardage requirements listed for quilt backings are calculated for 43"/44"w fabric. Using 90"w or 108"w fabric for the backing of a bed-sized quilt may eliminate piecing. To piece a backing using 43"/44"w fabric, use the following instructions.*

1. Measure length and width of quilt top; add 8" to each measurement.
2. If determined width is 79" or less, cut backing fabric into two lengths slightly longer than determined *length* measurement. Trim selvages. Place lengths with right sides facing and sew long edges together, forming tube (FIG. 16). Match seams and press along one fold (FIG. 17). Cut along pressed fold to form single piece (FIG. 18).
3. If determined width is more than 79", it may require less fabric yardage if the backing is pieced horizontally. Divide determined *length* measurement by 40" to determine how many widths will be needed. Cut required number of widths the determined *width* measurement. Trim selvages. Sew long edges together to form single piece.
4. Trim backing to size determined in Step 1; press seam allowances open.

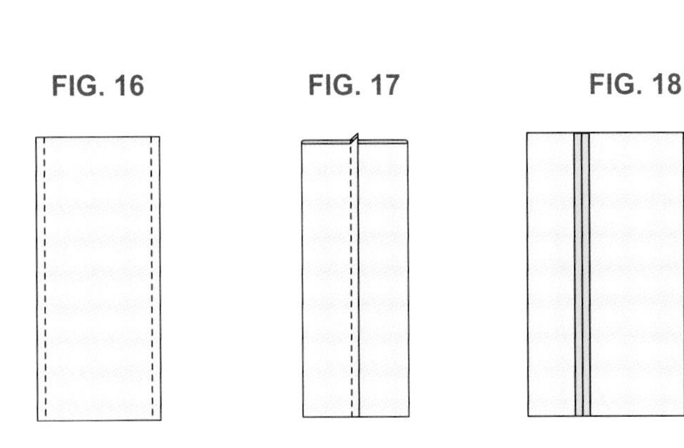

FIG. 16 FIG. 17 FIG. 18

choosing the batting

The appropriate batting will make quilting easier. For fine hand quilting, choose low-loft batting. All cotton or cotton/polyester blend battings work well for machine quilting because the cotton helps "grip" quilt layers. If quilt is to be tied, a high-loft batting, sometimes called extra-loft or fat batting, may be used to make the quilt "fluffy."

Types of batting include cotton, polyester, wool, cotton/polyester blend, cotton/wool blend, and silk.

When selecting batting, refer to package labels for characteristics and care instructions. Cut batting same size as prepared backing.

assembling the quilt

1. Examine wrong side of quilt top closely; trim any seam allowances and clip any threads that may show through front of the quilt. Press quilt top, being careful not to "set" any marked quilting lines.
2. Place backing *wrong* side up on flat surface. Use masking tape to tape edges of backing to surface. Place batting on top of backing fabric. Smooth batting gently, being careful not to stretch or tear. Center quilt top *right* side up on batting.
3. Use 1" rustproof safety pins to "pin-baste" all layers together, spacing pins approximately 4" apart. Begin at center and work toward outer edges to secure all layers. If possible, place pins away from areas that will be quilted, although pins may be removed as needed when quilting.

machine quilting methods

Use general-purpose thread in bobbin. Do not use quilting thread. Thread the needle of machine with general-purpose thread or transparent monofilament thread to make quilting blend with quilt top fabrics. Use decorative thread, such as a metallic or contrasting-color general-purpose thread, to make quilting lines stand out more.

straight-line quilting

The term "straight-line" is somewhat deceptive, since curves (especially gentle ones) as well as straight lines can be stitched with this technique.

1. Set stitch length for six to ten stitches per inch and attach walking foot to sewing machine.
2. Determine which section of quilt will have longest continuous quilting line, oftentimes area from center top to center bottom. Roll up and secure each edge of quilt to help reduce the bulk, keeping fabrics smooth. Smaller projects may not need to be rolled.
3. Begin stitching on longest quilting line, using very short stitches for the first 1/4" to "lock" quilting. Stitch across project, using one hand on each side of walking foot to slightly spread fabric and to guide fabric through machine. Lock stitches at end of quilting line.
4. Continue machine quilting, stitching longer quilting lines first to stabilize quilt before moving on to other areas.

free-motion quilting

Free-motion quilting may be free form or may follow a marked pattern.

1. Attach darning foot to sewing machine and lower or cover feed dogs.
2. Position quilt under darning foot; lower foot. Holding top thread, take a stitch and pull bobbin thread to top of quilt. To "lock" beginning of quilting line, hold top and bobbin threads while making three to five stitches in place.
3. Use one hand on each side of darning foot to slightly spread fabric and to move fabric through the machine. Even stitch length is achieved by using smooth, flowing hand motion and steady machine speed. Slow machine speed and fast hand movement will create long stitches. Fast machine speed and slow hand movement will create short stitches. Move quilt sideways, back and forth, in a circular motion, or in a random motion to create desired designs; do not rotate quilt. Lock stitches at end of each quilting line.

making a hanging sleeve

Attaching a hanging sleeve to back of wall hanging or quilt before the binding is added allows the project to be displayed on a wall.

1. Measure width of quilt top edge and subtract 1". Cut piece of fabric 7"w by determined measurement.
2. Press short edges of fabric piece 1/4" to wrong side; press edges 1/4" to wrong side again and machine stitch in place.
3. Matching wrong sides, fold piece in half lengthwise to form tube.
4. Follow project instructions to sew binding to quilt top and to trim backing and batting. Before Blindstitching binding to backing, match raw edges and stitch hanging sleeve to center top edge on back of quilt.
5. Finish binding quilt, treating hanging sleeve as part of backing.
6. Blindstitch bottom of hanging sleeve to backing, taking care not to stitch through to front of quilt.

FIG. 19

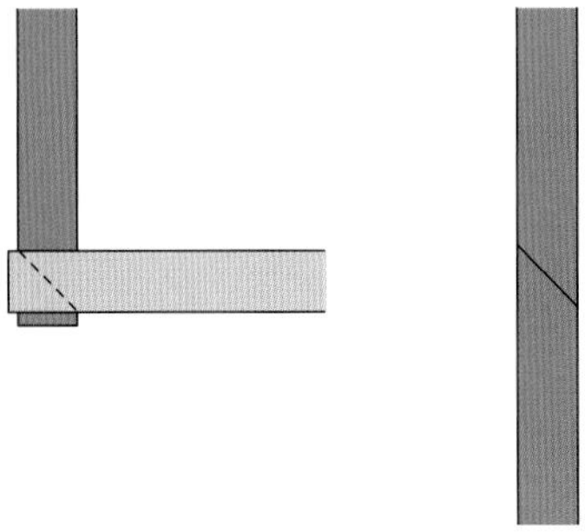

FIG. 20

FIG. 20a

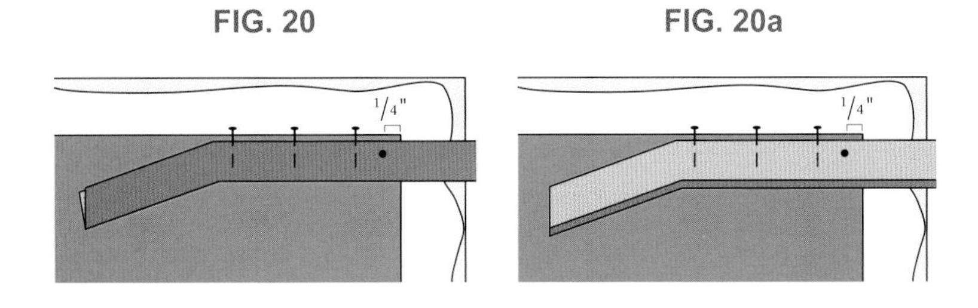

FIG. 21

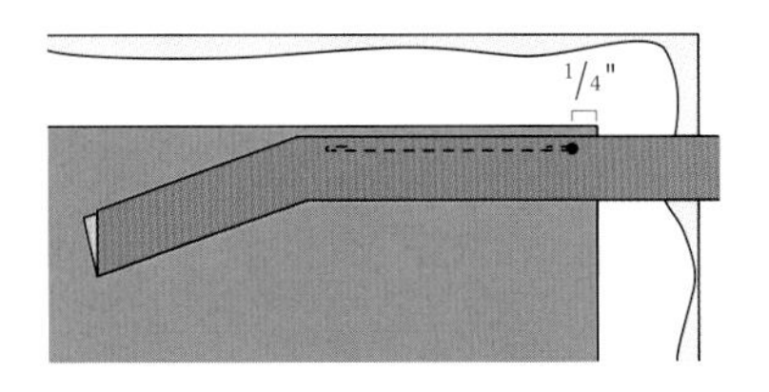

FIG. 22

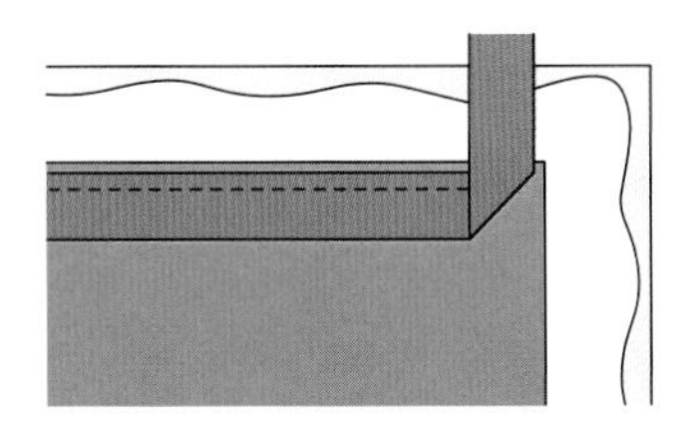

FIG. 23

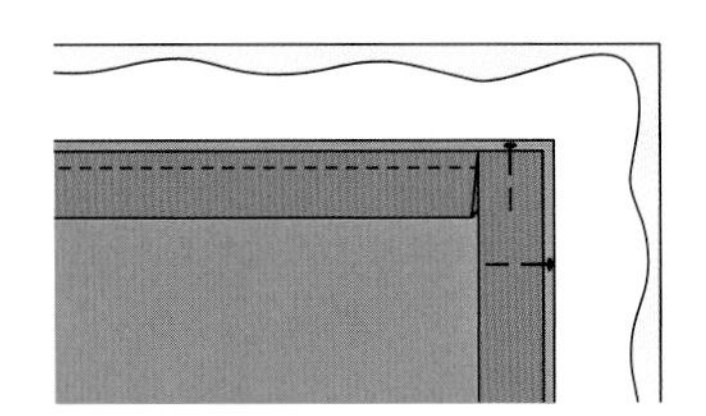

binding

making single-fold binding

1. With right sides together and using diagonal seams (FIG. 19), sew the short ends of the binding strips together.
2. Press seam allowances open. Press one long edge of binding $^1/_4$" to the wrong side.

making double-fold binding

1. With right sides together and using diagonal seams (FIG. 19), sew the short ends of the binding strips together.
2. Press seam allowances open. Matching wrong sides and raw edges, press strip(s) in half lengthwise to complete binding.

attaching binding

***Note:** Figs. 20-31 show attaching Double-Fold Binding. Single-Fold Binding is attached in the same manner, but will appear as shown in Fig. 20a.*

1. Beginning with one end near center on bottom edge of quilt, lay binding around quilt to make sure that seams in binding will not end up at a corner. Adjust placement if necessary. Matching raw edges of binding to raw edge of quilt top, pin binding to right side of quilt along one edge.
2. When you reach first corner, mark $^1/_4$" from corner of quilt top (FIG. 20).
3. Beginning approximately 10" from end of binding and using a $^1/_4$" seam allowance, sew binding to quilt, backstitching at beginning of stitching and at mark (FIG. 21). Lift needle out of fabric and clip thread.
4. Fold binding as shown in FIGS. 22 – 23 and pin binding to adjacent side, matching raw edges. When you've reached the next corner, mark $^1/_4$" from edge of quilt top.

5. Backstitching at edge of quilt top, sew pinned binding to quilt (FIG. 24); backstitch at the next mark. Lift needle out of fabric and clip thread.
6. Continue sewing binding to quilt, stopping approximately 10" from starting point (FIG. 25).
7. Bring beginning and end of binding to center of opening and fold each end back, leaving a 1/4" space between folds (FIG. 26). Finger press folds.
8. Unfold ends of binding and draw a line across wrong side in finger-pressed crease. Draw a line through the lengthwise pressed fold of binding at the same spot to create a cross mark. With edge of ruler at cross mark, line up 45° angle marking on ruler with one long side of binding. Draw a diagonal line from edge to edge. Repeat on remaining end, making sure that the two diagonal lines are angled the same way (FIG. 27).
9. Matching right sides and diagonal lines, pin binding ends together at right angles (FIG. 28).
10. Machine stitch along diagonal line (FIG. 29), removing pins as you stitch.
11. Lay binding against quilt to double check that it is correct length.
12. Trim binding ends, leaving a 1/4" seam allowance; press seam open. Stitch binding to quilt.
13. Trim backing and batting a scant 1/4" larger than quilt top so that batting and backing will fill the binding when it is folded over to quilt backing.

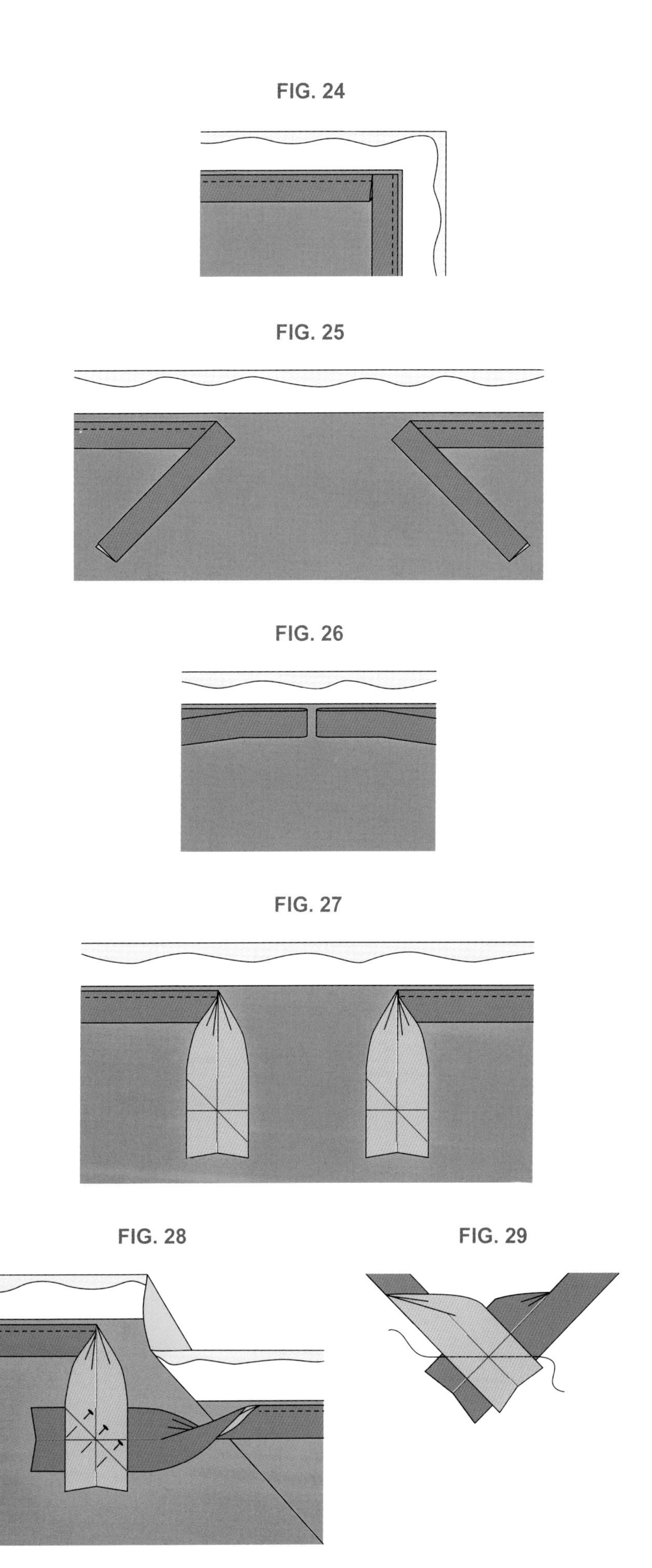
FIG. 24

FIG. 25

FIG. 26

FIG. 27

FIG. 28

FIG. 29

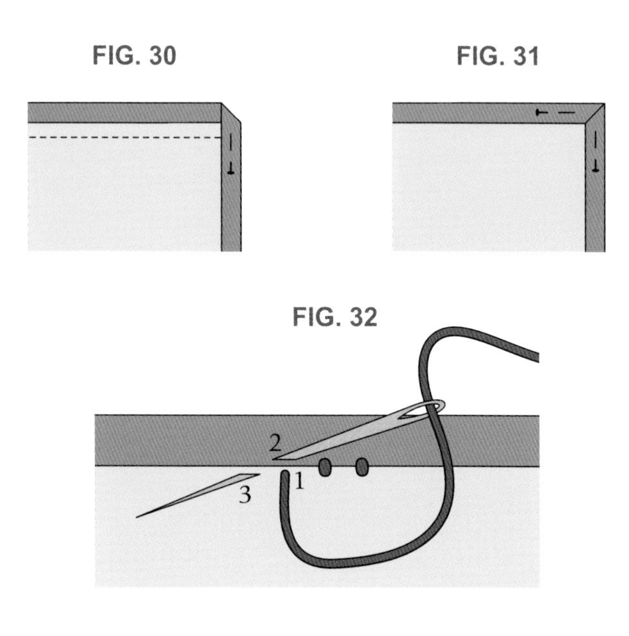

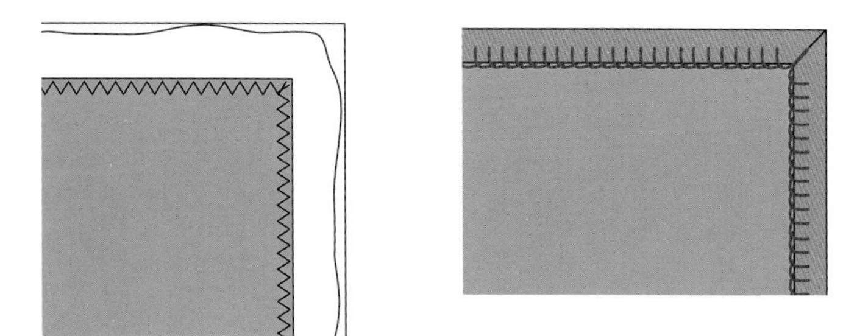

14. On one edge of quilt, fold binding over to quilt backing and pin pressed edge in place, covering stitching line (FIG. 30). On adjacent side, fold binding over, forming a mitered corner (FIG. 31). Repeat to pin remainder of binding in place.
15. Blindstitch binding to backing, taking care not to stitch through to front of quilt.

blind stitch

Come up at 1, go down at 2, and come up at 3 (FIG. 32). Length of stitches may be varied as desired.

pat's machine-sewn binding

*For a quick and easy finish when attaching straight-grain binding, Pat sews her binding to the **back** of the quilt and **Machine Blanket Stitches** or Straight Stitches it in place on the front, eliminating all hand stitching. Refer to **Machine Appliqué**, page 72, for Blanket Stitch technique.*

1. Using a narrow zigzag, stitch around quilt close to the raw edges (FIG. 33). Trim backing and batting even with edges of quilt top.
2. Beginning with one end near center on bottom edge of quilt, lay binding around quilt to make sure that seams in binding will not end up at a corner. Adjust placement if necessary. Matching raw edges of binding to raw edge of quilt top, pin binding to the ***backing*** side of quilt along one edge.
3. Follow Steps 2-14 of **Attaching Binding**, page 76, folding binding over to quilt front. Machine Blanket Stitch or Topstitch binding close to pressed edge (FIG. 34).

Many thanks go to these ladies for
their beautiful work:

Welcome to the Neighborhood
pieced by Larcie Burnett and
quilted by Cindy Dickinson,
Pinkpaw and Company

Boardwalk
pieced by Nelwyn Gray and
quilted by Cindy Dickinson,
Pinkpaw and Company

Bozley's Triangles
pieced and quilted by Sue Graham

Pretty Plates
pieced and quilted by Lina LaMora

I Remember
pieced by Nelwyn Gray and
quilted by Cindy Dickinson,
Pinkpaw and Company

Thanks to P&B Textiles, Andover Fabrics, and Moda for many of the beautiful fabrics featured in these projects and to Bernina for providing my sewing machine. To make the projects I used Aurifil® thread, Mountain Mist® batting, and HeatnBond Lite® fusible web.

Metric Conversion Chart

Inches x 2.54 = centimeters (cm)	Yards x .9144 = meters (m)
Inches x 25.4 = millimeters (mm)	Yards x 91.44 = centimeters (cm)
Inches x .0254 = meters (m)	Centimeters x .3937 = inches (")
	Meters x 1.0936 = yards (yd)

Standard Equivalents

1/8"	3.2 mm	0.32 cm	1/8 yard	11.43 cm	0.11 m
1/4"	6.35 mm	0.635 cm	1/4 yard	22.86 cm	0.23 m
3/8"	9.5 mm	0.95 cm	3/8 yard	34.29 cm	0.34 m
1/2"	12.7 mm	1.27 cm	1/2 yard	45.72 cm	0.46 m
5/8"	15.9 mm	1.59 cm	5/8 yard	57.15 cm	0.57 m
3/4"	19.1 mm	1.91 cm	3/4 yard	68.58 cm	0.69 m
7/8"	22.2 mm	2.22 cm	7/8 yard	80 cm	0.8 m
1"	25.4 mm	2.54 cm	1 yard	91.44 cm	0.91 m